Clash of Titans:
Atlas Shrugged, John Galt & Jesus Christ

By

Chad Brand
Tom Pratt

To Our Children and Grandchildren

For the World they will Inherit

Chad

Tashia, Owen, Cassandra

Katelyn, Cora, Madison, Keira, Kameron, Buck

Tom

Tom, III and Dale

Table of Contents

Acknowledgments

This a book about a book, as well as an author, that takes a negative stance toward Christian faith and its truth claims. It is not often that people like your present authors recommend the serious reading of such writings to the general public and especially to that of professed Christian believers. In this case we make a resounding exception. Read *Atlas Shrugged*! Read it carefully and thoroughly and enjoy its drama and mystery and romance, but whatever you do, read it through and ponder its "message" in light of current events. However, a warning is in order about the book you have before you. It reveals a lot of the plot in some detail and quotes extensively from its pages. The purpose in our doing so is to encourage the casual reader of reviews and summaries to get beyond what you may have heard and read and buy and read the book itself before you make up your mind about its relationship to traditional Christian themes. It is an important work about a very contemporary subject that deserves more than a casual dismissal as some atheist's hatchet job on Christianity. Our experience has been that without knowing and understanding the context of Ayn Rand's philosophy enfleshed in *Atlas Shrugged*, many Christians have reacted negatively, with unhappy consequences, to truth that could not be conveyed in any other way than Rand has done it.

Ayn Rand, as we explain at least briefly, came of age in the Soviet political slave-camp nation established in Russia in 1917. She was influenced by the tradition of Eastern Orthodox Christianity and takes her understanding of Christianity from that milieu. Her literary tradition is Russian, and she was of the conviction that great ideas require more than abstract speculative explication to communicate real understanding. They require the concrete portrayal of the novel to make them come to life. This is the tradition of *Atlas Shrugged* and her other works of fiction. She wanted the masses of people to read and understand her philosophy in its actual working environment. With that in mind we have used lots of her own words and scenes to hopefully accomplish what we would not have been able to otherwise—pique the interest of those who may be predisposed to simply ignore or excoriate her work in a way that propositional statements and

6

discussion of her ideas will not suffice to do. Furthermore, in today's atmosphere of hostility to evangelically oriented Christianity many are wondering with the old line in the movie 'Marathon Man,' "Is it safe?" Yes it is! And we hope the contextualization we have sought in lengthy quotations highlights this fact.

We have also written this book for another audience—those who wholeheartedly or at least agnostically embrace Rand's atheism and distrust of Christianity. It is our hope that you may find something here that will cause you to investigate further the truth claims of Christian faith and find them not as formidable to the rational mind as you have been led to believe. We think Ayn Rand was familiar intimately with only one strain of Christian tradition and did not have a full grasp on the rational basis for faith in the Western traditions. We cannot know her mind, but we do know from what is written in the speeches of characters in *Atlas Shrugged* and her other works that misconceptions are apparent. If you are one of those who has only dipped superficially into Christian thought and the Bible, we invite you to read this book and make yourself a binding promise to investigate thoroughly who Jesus Christ is and what He has done for this material world and all its inhabitants.

But be warned one and all—if you are put off by knowing too much of the plot ahead of time, read the book first and then read this one for the discussion of its implications for Christian faith. *Atlas* has been around long enough now that many already know the gist of its argument and the plot and will do just fine reading this analysis first. The book is long enough and the plot is labyrinthine enough and the philosophical speeches intricate enough that we think what we have done will just build your interest in reading the whole 1200 pages. But consider yourself forewarned.

We acknowledge here the helpful work of others in filling in the holes of our personal knowledge of Rand's life and times and the process she followed in constructing her characters and plot lines. Of particular help here have been Jennifer Burns, Anne Heller, and the compilation and editing of Edward Younkins, all of which are cited in the notes. Donald Luskin and Andrew Greta are very helpful in setting forth the contemporary parallels to the setting in the novel. David Kotter has authored a paper on some issues of Christian faith and practice relative to Rand's work, which we also cite, and there is a website for seeing more of his work. In addition we have reviewed for information the DVD from Virgil Films and Entertainment, "Ayn Rand & the Prophecy of *Atlas Shrugged*," available on Amazon, as well as the film of "The Fountainhead" starring Gary Cooper as Howard Roark. We have seen also the first part of "Atlas Shrugged" on DVD and recommend it as well. All these sources are available for the interested reader, and we have found them very helpful in writing this book. Which is to say that this literary work is a product of many contributions from other sources, but that implies no endorsement on the part of any of them. What you have here is our opinion from the perspective of what some call "fans," but we hope that doesn't discourage your taking a little walk with us through a work of fiction that reads like today's news.

Unless otherwise noted, all citations from *Atlas Shrugged* are from the Centennial Edition using Kindle for Mac.

Introduction

Who is John Galt? If you know the answer to that question, you are at least among the curious who have investigated a book that today stands next to the Bible and Scott Peck's *The Road Less Traveled* in terms of its influence on people's lives. (According to a 1991 survey done for the Library of Congress and Book-of-the-Month Club [with] 5,000 Book-of-the-Month club members surveyed, with a "large gap existing between the #1 book and the rest of the list".) Ayn Rand's *Atlas Shrugged* has fascinated and shocked and dismayed readers for 55 years and today is once again on pundits' lips and in headlines across the US during presidential election season. Today it stands in the top fifty of sales on Amazon and sold 500,000 copies worldwide in 2009, with comparable numbers in 2011 and is still on the *New York Times* bestseller list.

Rush Limbaugh, Glenn Beck, Judge Clarence Thomas, several Congressmen, and now vice-presidential candidate Paul Ryan are among those that have recommended the book, though Ryan has sought at times to distance himself from his endorsement. On the other hand, former Enron consultant and now leftist *New York Times* economic pundit Paul Krugman has blogged: "There are two novels that can change a bookish fourteen-year-old's life: *The Lord of the Rings* and *Atlas Shrugged*. One is a childish fantasy that often engenders a lifelong obsession with its unbelievable heroes, leading to an emotionally stunted, socially crippled adulthood, unable to deal with the real world. The other, of course, involves orcs."[1] For many who read the book years ago (with periodic re-reads) today's economic and political news stories have eerie similarities to the fictionalized world Ms. Rand created so long ago, "in a galaxy far, far away" (?), a possibility suggested by some who have reviewed the book as science fiction.

President Barack Obama seems to be playing a role out of the novel with his "Mr. business man…you didn't build that" talk. And congressional leadership

---

[1] For the best take on Krugman the economic leftist, see Donald Luskin & Andrew Greta, *I Am John Galt: Today's Heroic Innovators Building the World and the Villainous Parasites Destroying It* (New York: John Wiley and Sons, Kindle Edition, 2011), Chapter 2.

from both sides of the aisles seem bent on playing their parts with a Senate that refuses even to pass a budget for three years and a House that flips and flops, depending on the direction of political winds, between authorizing spending and raising or lowering taxes or doing nothing at all, but always, always, always protecting "earmarks" for their cronies. Massive public debt threatens to swamp the greatest economy in the history of the world, and the nation is more and more divided between those who work and pay income taxes and those who work and pay no income taxes and those who simply go from one government agency to the next with a hand out expecting more, or worse yet, camp out in the streets of major cities in lawless "squattervilles" of filth, drunkenness, and crime. In the approaching emergency of debt and entitlement the Obama campaign declares "we can't wait" as his czars (35 or so of them at last count) issue directives for regulation and favoritism to various groups, financial institutions, and businesses. At the very least Ayn Rand deserves an "A" for prescience of a sort usually reserved for the messengers of Yahweh in Scripture. Luskin's suggested parallels in the book cited above (including parallels to Steve Jobs, Bill Gates, Krugman, Alan Greenspan, Barney Frank, Henry Waxman and others) are apt and devastating at times.

Of course, statements like that haul a whole lot more baggage into the equation, and that's what this little book is about. The Christian world of those called "evangelicals," a term not so easily defined as it once was, is not really prepared for a discussion of the values of John Galt and Dagny Taggart as they impact a Christian's economic and political thinking. We believe it is time to speak more extensively and directly from a biblical Christian perspective to the issues Ayn Rand and others are raising. Our search for any such treatment has turned up very little beyond the occasional column or blog and the simple discounting of what appears on the surface to be little more than the hopeless diatribe of a misguided and tragic writer/philosopher from a dated and unappealing thought world. "Hateful" is not an uncommon evaluation, as are "un-feeling" and "un-Christian." John Galt is sometimes labeled "anti-Christ." "Immorality" is, of course, a regular pejorative relating to occasional sexual content. And, always, the elephant in the front room is "atheistic." But perhaps most obvious is the sheer

10

disbelief that anyone could seriously conceive of a world so darkened with the selfish "egoism" (Rand's central moral code, about which more later) of "heroes" unmoved by the pleas of others for pity and altruism. We do seem to live in a christianized cocoon of soft moralism and ethical mysticism.

In the world of the non-religious the book has been widely panned from the beginning. The book was dismissed by some as "a homage to greed", while late author Gore Vidal described its philosophy as "nearly perfect in its immorality." Helen Beal Woodward, reviewing *Atlas Shrugged* for *The Saturday Review*, opined that the novel was written with "dazzling virtuosity" but that it was "shot through with hatred." This was echoed by Granville Hicks, writing for *The New York Times Book Review*, who also stated that the book was "written out of hate." The reviewer for *Time* magazine asked: "Is it a novel? Is it a nightmare? Is it Superman – in the comic strip or the Nietzschean version?" In the magazine *National Review*, Whittaker Chambers called *Atlas Shrugged* "sophomoric" and "remarkably silly," and said it "can be called a novel only by devaluing the term." Chambers argued against the novel's implicit endorsement of atheism, whereby "Randian man, like Marxian man is made the center of a godless world." Chambers also wrote that the implicit message of the novel is akin to "Hitler's National Socialism and Stalin's brand of Communism" ("To a gas chamber — go!").[2] Donald Luskin in his *I Am John Galt* refers to the Chambers review as "a smear."[3] Recently, Jason Lee Steorts of *National Review* used the word "ghastly" to refer to Rand's relentless pursuit of the consequences of failure to stem the tide of the march of the "looters," one of her favorite characterizations of the cadre of legalized predators upon the production of others.[4] Additionally, Marvin Olasky has warned those who would commend Rand's thought for Christian consumption that they should specify carefully what they would recommend and what they would critique.[5] We intend to follow as best we can this injunction.

---

[2] Opinions herein from the Wikipedia site.

[3] Ibid., 7.

[4] *National Review*, August 23, 2010.

[5] Marvin Olasky, "Take a Stand Against Rand," *WORLDmag.com*, July 16, 2011.

Your authors here have read the book (between them) numerous times and had discussions over the years about its implications. We have authored the current e-book from Kregel, *Awaiting the City* and the fuller treatment in binding and electronic version to be out in the Spring of 2013, *Seeking the City*, both of which seek to address biblically, theologically, historically, and politically the current state of political economy in the West. We have many years of experience in business and church and theological education and feel compelled to weigh in on Rand's idealized world of heroic producers and slovenly moochers and looters. Our plan is fairly simple: First, we will relate a bit of the pertinent data from the life and philosophy of the author as it relates to issues of concern to professed Christians. Then, we will review briefly the story of *Atlas Shrugged*, keeping in mind that such outlines are numerous in the world of the internet. Further, we will raise one by one several specific issues that are at the center of the book's argument (for that is what Rand intended it to be—she wrote the novel rather than a full philosophical treatise) with a view to a specifically biblical and theological assessment and critique.

Along this short walk around a massive novel we will be addressing the following issues specifically and others as side-paths: Aristotelian logic, objectivism, mysticism, the human mind and rational thought, the meaning of money, capitalism and political economy, the affirmation of life in a culture of death, altruism, the place of the individual in society and biblical theology, the virtue of "self-ishness," and of course, the contrast and likeness between John Galt and Jesus Christ.

One of the things your authors have learned over time is that the cliché, "Truth is where you find it" is, well, true! We recommend *Atlas Shrugged* as being worth the trouble to read and absorb for a number of reasons, not least of which is that we all benefit from the various ways our minds connect to our own worldview and that of others. Seldom is a walk through the forest like this completely unprofitable. Rand's *magnum opus* tests one's patience at times and seems shocking and fantastic to some sensibilities.[6] But any serious assessment of her work must take into account its glaring and uncanny accuracy in today's climate of failing socialistic democracies and market-oriented crony capitalism. A hinge of history may well be turning before our eyes. Rand visualized it more than half a century ago when she said: "We are fast approaching the stage of the ultimate inversion: the stage where the government is free to do anything it pleases, while the citizens may act only by permission; which is the stage of the darkest periods of human history, the stage of rule by brute force."

In the hope and prayer that this will not prove so just yet, we offer this alert to would-be followers of Jesus the Messiah.

---

[6] Watching recently the first installment of the film from Hollywood re-enforces this sense that we are in a world of almost science fiction.

Chapter 1 - What Is Atlas Shrugged?

In the heart of New York City stands a sculpture of the Titan, Atlas, holding up a massive representation of the heavens above the planet on which it stands. Weighing more than 15 tons and standing 45 feet high, it was erected during the depths of the Great Depression (1937), the time frame for Ayn Rand's first success as a novelist, and was intended to convey an impression of the ancient Graeco-Roman myth about a conflict between the Titans, ruled by Cronus, and the Olympians led by Zeus, the rebel against Cronus, who had become weakened in old age. Upon the defeat of the Titans Zeus sentenced Atlas, their leader, to a life of holding up the heavens. The various mythologies relate his struggle and suffering under that load. Rand eventually chose the title for her novel on the advice of her husband. She had worked on her *magnum opus* under the title, "The Strike," for years, while "Atlas Shrugged" was only a chapter title. But reflection on what Atlas might have done in a different mythology led to the suggestion that he might have "shrugged" off the load as if on strike.

"Atlas" means "he who dares or suffers" and is verbally cognate with "atlantis," (the name given to the more prosaic "Galt's Gulch" in the novel) the name of the mythical city intended to counter Plato's conception of the ideal society in *The Republic*. "Rand's choice of Atlantis as a symbol for her utopia of liberated producers may also be directed in part against Plato. The first recorded reference to (and probably invention of) the legend of Atlantis occurs in Plato's dialogues Timceus [sic] and Critius, where Atlantis is explicitly introduced (TimWus 17c-27b; Critics 1 1 Oc-1 14c) as the enemy of a city organized along the lines of Plato's Republic-thus making Atlantis the original anti-Platonic society' (...Plato identifies Atlas as the first ruler of Atlantis: Critius 114a)."[7] Rand considered Plato to be "the godfather of Communism."[8] It is also most noteworthy

---

[7] Kirsti Minsaas, "Ayn Rand's Recasting of Ancient Myths in Atlas Shrugged," in Edward W. Younkins, *Ayn Rand's Atlas Shrugged: A Philosophical and Literary Companion* (Kindle Locations 1380-1383).

[8] Jennifer Burns, *Goddess of the Market: Ayn Rand and the American Right* (New York: Oxford University Press, 2009), 109.

that the brother of Atlas was Prometheus (who sided with Zeus in the rebellion against Cronus), the one sentenced, because of offenses (stealing fire from the gods and giving it to men) to Zeus, to be chained to a rock in the Caucasus as bait to the scavengers and have his liver picked over daily. This mythology about the suffering of heroic rebels against the tyranny of the gods is a common theme in the ancient mythological world. Out of this matrix of mythology and historical development in the West an immortal (almost) title was born. And a massive following through 55 years and counting continues to make the title profitable and compelling.

Ayn Rand was born Alissa Zinovievna Rosenbaum in St. Petersburg, Russia, on February 2, 1905. At age six, she taught herself to read and two years later discovered her first fictional hero in a French magazine for children, thus capturing the heroic vision which sustained her throughout her life. At the age of nine, she decided to make fiction-writing her career. Thoroughly opposed to the mysticism and collectivism of Russian culture, she thought of herself as a European writer, especially after encountering authors such as Walter Scott and (in 1918) Victor Hugo, the writer she most admired. During her high school years, she was eyewitness to both the Kerensky Revolution, which she supported, and (in 1917) the Bolshevik Revolution, which she denounced from the outset. This is the fateful hour of the arrival in reality of the Marxist slogan "from each according to his ability to each according to his need," an idea whose trail of blood and sorrow seems to be never ending. More on this later.

In order to escape the fighting, which she experienced firsthand when her family's pharmacy was invaded and confiscated by soldiers of the revolution, her family fled to the Crimea, where she finished high school. The final Communist victory and the confiscation of her father's pharmacy brought on periods of near-starvation. During this period she confirmed with a entry in her journal that she was an atheist.[9] When introduced to American history in her last year of high school, she immediately took America as her model of what a nation of free men

---

[9] Jeffrey Britting, *Ayn Rand* (New York: Overlook Hardcover, 2004), 16. Citation from a paper by David S. Kotter of Indiana Wesleyan University. Further articles on economics are available at **www.davidkotter.com**.

could be. When her family returned from the Crimea, she entered the University of Petrograd to study philosophy and history. During this period her father was allowed to rebuild his business, but it was promptly confiscated again. His response was to declare himself "on strike" in refusal to work. His wife Anna seems to have been able to work odd jobs without interference and confiscations and the family managed to survive.

Graduating in 1924, Alissa experienced the disintegration of free inquiry and the take-over of the university by communist thugs. Amidst the increasingly gray life, her one great pleasure was Western films and plays. Long a movie fan, she entered the State Institute for Cinema Arts in 1924 to study screen-writing. In late 1925, she obtained permission to leave the USSR for a visit to relatives in the United States. Although she told Soviet authorities that her visit would be short, she was determined never to return to Russia. Arriving in New York City in February 1926, she spent six months with her relatives in Chicago, obtained extensions to her visa, and then left for Hollywood to pursue a career as a screenwriter.[10] It was at this time she changed her name to Ayn Rand. Her Hollywood connections would prove invaluable over the years as the source of income and eventually real wealth.

Her first novel, *We the Living*, was published in 1936 following a long period of rejection by the publishing establishment in the US and Great Britain. This was the time period known as "the Red Decade" for intellectuals and various cultural elites of the period.[11] The book is her most autobiographical and details the dreary death-in-life of the Soviet system. This opinion was not welcomed in the age of the New Deal, whose leadership was enamored of the planned economy upheld in the myths of Soviet propaganda and much of the media in the West at the time. A shorter work, *Anthem*, an anti-collectivist yarn appeared in 1937. She

---

[10] Information in these paragraphs on biographical information may be found in Ayn Rand, *Atlas Shrugged* (Centennial Edition) Plume. Kindle Edition loc. 26,800. See also Burns, *Goddess of the Market,* and Anne C. Heller, *Ayn Rand and the World She Made* (New York: Random House, 2009).

[11] See Eugene Lyons, *The Red Decade: The Stalinist Penetration of America* (New York: Bobbs Merrill, 1941).

followed this with *The Fountainhead* in 1943, after having been rejected by twelve publishers. The book became a bestseller by word of mouth, a positive review in the *New York Times* and positive comments about Rand herself from the respected Isabel Paterson, and succeeded in making Rand the champion of individualism among the *cognocenti* of the day and thousands of ordinary readers in years to follow. *Atlas Shrugged* was begun in 1946 and published in 1957 as a response to requests for a full rendering of her philosophy. It is generally accepted by reviewers and students of her work that this is her crowning achievement and contains the idealized essence of Objectivism concretized rather than discussed in the abstract. As such, it uses as a vehicle what has been labeled "an intellectual mystery story that integrated ethics, metaphysics, epistemology, politics, economics, and sex."[12] This is an apt summary statement that defines the moral parameters of Rand's intent in writing the novel. Consequently one should not be surprised to find epic-style speeches and idealized conversations that do not occur normally in every day interchanges. Strangely, many critics have seen fit to denigrate the writing style and storytelling for this use of the vehicle. It seems to us that once the purpose is understood, it is best to just jump on for the 1200 page ride.

In her own words Rand frankly states her straightforward philosophy: "My philosophy, in essence, is the concept of man as a heroic being, with his own happiness as the moral purpose of his life, with productive achievement as his noblest activity, and reason as his only absolute."[13] She allowed that she owed nothing in her own theories to anyone but Aristotle, with whom she had many disagreements, but whose "definition of the laws of logic and of the means of human knowledge is so great an achievement that his errors are irrelevant by comparison." In tribute to that sentiment each major section uses one of his assertions as a title—"Non-contradiction," "Either-Or" and "A is A." She was an atheist, though she was deeply influenced by Isabel Paterson (who did believe in God) a writer and critic who was flatly opposed to governmental usurpation of

---

[12] Ibid., loc. 26,831.

[13] Ibid., loc. 26,784.

power in any area other than the prevention of force and fraud. Paterson opposed not only Rooseveltian New Deal power grabs but those of Hoover Republicans as well. Rand acknowledged the influence of Paterson in her life, though she later broke with her mentor.[14]

Rand confessed to a lifelong search for the "ideal man," first projected heroically and stoically in *The Fountainhead* (Howard Roark) and elaborated on at length in the character of John Galt. Roark was a portrait of the man in himself, and Galt was an expansion of the mission of such a man who refused any longer to be used by the "looters" of business and government. She claimed to have met and married (1929) such a man in Frank O'Connor, to whom she was married for 50 years. That relationship was influenced by her relationship with another man, Nathaniel Branden,[15] with whom she had on ongoing relationship (after consent from the spouses of both parties) until 1968. She and O'Connor appeared to have mended their marriage after much conflict and O'Connor's bouts with alcoholism subsided. He died in 1979. Rand followed him in death in 1982. She and O'Connor had no children. More on the subject of sexuality and the absence of children in Rand's work later.

This is the human background to *Atlas Shrugged*. It is important for our subject because she contended that her philosophy was about how to live on earth. She was clear that this was all there was or is; so much the more therefore do we need to LIVE now. Her heroic characters continually affirm life and its best value (to them), happiness in productivity and the corollary of rejoicing in the productivity of others through fair trade-offs of one productive effort for the other. They pay a heavy price for their credo, however, for they suffer at the hands of those who would coerce them into a productivity that is put in the service of coercive societal demands. Consequently, the conflict seen in the mythological

---

[14] Stephen Cox, "Atlas and 'the Bible': Rand's Debt to Isabel Paterson," in Edward W. Younkins, *Ayn Rand's Atlas Shrugged: A Philosophical and Literary Companion*, Kindle Edition, loc. 4725-4785.

[15] She and Branden collaborated for years on her work until she abruptly broke off the entire relationship.

18

experiences of Atlas and Prometheus and others becomes the foil for stating and developing the morality to which her heroes aspire—for theirs is not an amoral world at all. To seek to coerce from another anything involuntary is an act of death-dealing. The first one to use force is the ultimate criminal, no matter what he uses as his justification or what the object of his coercive effort is. One might defend oneself or other innocents from this use, but one may never initiate the use of force. Fraud, of course, is a form of force through subterfuge and must be defended against. This is the legitimate exercise of governmental power—the prevention of fraud and force from damaging or taking the life of individuals and/or overwhelming societal structures. The underlying premise and conflict in *Atlas Shrugged* is that government has usurped the life and happiness of the individual by becoming itself the purveyor of fraud and force in the marketplace where man must be able to use the results of his own productivity to survive, to live. Moreover, that usurpation and reversal of morality has been dressed in the garb of altruism (we will deal at some length with this concept later) with a view to enlisting the victims of its immorality in the overall fraudulent exercise. The conflict at the heart of the novel concerns the decision of one man to stop the process by cutting off its motive power, seen as the mind of man made free to invent and produce and enjoy the fruits of his labors. How he goes about this task is the plot line and the philosophical construct of Rand's work.

The "happiness" to which she refers in our summary quotation above can only be achieved by the virtuous person. It cannot be found through living a dissolute life or living at the expense or for the happiness of others. It is most clearly derived from creative effort of the mind applied to the material world of living and working. One cannot expect another person to bring happiness to himself, and it is immoral to regard it as another's duty to do so. The happiness experienced in community or fellowship of human beings is that of equals who derive pleasure from experiencing the excellence of others in their pursuit of happiness or in the exchange of one material good or service for another through voluntary association. One might also, even must, experience happiness through aspiration toward the seemingly unattainable, either in oneself or in others—that is, rather than envy and/or resentment of the success and achievement of others as against one's own limitations, happiness is celebration of the exceptional creativity of the master at his or her craft and inspiration to one's own efforts. "Ayn Rand's heroes are larger-than-life projections of her ideals. They lead lives of virtue based on consistent personal convictions with a coherent philosophical system to guide them."[16] This is what makes them truly happy.

At the most simple level happiness is due appreciation and celebration of the ability to cook a wonderful meal (even a roadside diner hamburger, as the philosopher Hugh Akston does in the novel) or show complete competence at some craft or other learned and productive activity or service. At the highest level it is the ability to enjoy the creative genius of the inventor or the philosopher or the musician or the railroad builder or the scientist or any other of the pursuits that raise the level of happiness of all those around them. The ones who create in this fashion are, of course, the heroes of Rand's philosophy, and they comprise a small percentage of the general population. They should be admired and honored and imitated in their pure devotion to the productivity of the mind. Beyond that, as we shall further explore, all those who admire such heroes and emulate them in their own lives will also find happiness.

By contrast the immorality of the lazy and dissolute and misguided (who are both envious and unhappy) can be seen in the inability to discern the difference between creativity and its fruits and money. Money has meaning to Rand and her heroes only as it expresses what it takes to produce wealth. Otherwise it is merely paper with fraudulent printing on it. Not surprisingly her characters have no use for currency that is not backed by the actual value of gold, and wealth consists in the accumulation of the benefits of productive labor, not in the looting of others' goods. One cannot truly enjoy the nature of money as a means of exchange unless productivity and creativity have invested it with meaning outside its intrinsic nature. One's happiness is already achieved in the process of creating it, so dissipating it in slovenly activities such as casual sex and drunkenness or indulgent feasting and public spectacle actually defeat the goal of happiness that was

---

[16] Donald Luskin & Andrew Greta, 14.

20

achieved in the creation of wealth in the first place. Those who merely acquire money through various means of theft or fraudulent business or as a payoff for political favors and business cooperation in the destruction of competitors or as recipients of "benefits" not earned through labor and the application of the mind are the true "materialists," for their acquired money has no connection to productivity.

For Rand and her heroes the source of wealth creation and happiness through productivity is the human mind. It is not merely labor at any level. It is the mind of man applied to that which becomes a resource in their hands as he or she mold and shape the formless into that which is useful and gratifying and beautiful to themselves and others. They do not do it "for others" but for the personal satisfaction it brings, and they are gratified when others appreciate and applaud and most of all *understand* what it took to create their masterpieces, small and great. This is the realm of the "spiritual," and it cannot be divorced from the physical, for it cannot be experienced or expressed without the physical. To Randians the separation of soul from body, as the Enlightenment philosophers and theologians and scientists did, resulted in an immoral dichotomy. Man is not a "struggle between a corpse and a ghost," for man without a soul or spirit or mind is nothing but a corpse, and the mind or soul without a body is simply a ghost. Such a condition is actually death, not life, and one cannot be moral and not affirm life itself. So one must seek out those who affirm life in order to have a community that is moral in its ethos and relationships.

The nature of this community is expressed in the confession at the heart of Rand's philosophy: "I swear—by my life and my love of it—that I will never live for the sake of another man, nor ask another man to live for mine." This is the Golden Rule of Rand's philosophy; the code of Galt's Gulch. The emphasis in her ideal is on the word "live." It is irrational to believe that men and women will actually *live* "for the sake of" others without reciprocal arrangements or subterfuges that provide, in effect, hide-outs from their inconsistencies. If they are honestly satisfied and happy in some reciprocal relationship, it is because the thing in itself makes them happiest, and they have gladly consented to provide reciprocity in that which reinforces the happiness of the other. This cannot be said to be "living for the sake of" another. It is living out one's own happiness in the joyful discovery of another's happiness, which is itself not derived from using another person's emotional capital.[17] If, on the other hand, one claims that the relationship is self-fulfilling while one is putting obligation upon the other for reciprocity, one is simply self-deceived and irrational. Worse, if one engages in relationships that supposedly flow from altruistic (more on this terminology later) motives and claims to be purely unselfish and even "sacrificial," one destroys and denigrates the true humanity of the other person for one's own gratification and happiness, thus irrationally annulling the very concept of sacrifice and altruism itself. Enslavement and degradation follow, especially as other parties size up the situation and play the game to their own advantage by sowing guilt and fear in the minds of the inattentive and unsuspecting. In Rand's works this is the pathway of the "looters" and "moochers," who people the halls of government and whose main henchmen are business men and women looking to capitalize on relationships at the expense of the merely creative and productive. Consequently, rational selfishness is the mark of moral people who examine life and its varied relationships with proper lenses in place and enter into relationships and transactions accordingly—that is, freely and with mutual benefit.

It should be clear from the foregoing that Rand struck a nerve when she advanced such radical thoughts without apology. The reason she was so straightforward, besides the sheer rational clarity with which she sought to think herself through to conclusions, is the discovery that is peculiar to her thought and most innovative of all. She believed, and her characters find themselves gradually being persuaded, that the world as we know it runs on the fuel of the guilty sufferings of the most creative and productive among us, whether they are the creator heroes or more ordinarily heroic and competent people, including mothers and cooks and managers and office assistants and track layers and station

---

[17] By now the reader should be able to discern that Rand does not speak of the kind of vacuous "happiness" bandied about in modern discourse. It might be analogous to that mentioned in the preamble to the US Constitution, but it is a weighty term in her philosophy. We will take up the subject of familial and fraternal relationship when we deal specifically with altruism.

22

managers and clerks and anyone else who affirms the primacy of life. That is, because the game has been rigged by the looters and moochers and manipulators (those that some have called "political entrepreneurs"). They require a kind of consent to their activities that will give cover to their nefarious schemes—the masses of the public unthinkingly going along in mob-like subservience and obsequious abetting. That is why the philosophies that depend upon altruistic rationales are immoral and evil. They discovered that the cloak of supposed unselfishness and sacrifice "for the common good" could be made to fit all but the most relentlessly rational among us. Moreover, one must be virtually stony-hearted to resist the pleas of the "needy" (here we/she speak of an inner state that may or may not be matched by an outward economic condition) for compassion (a willingness to suspend rationality in the face of deserved consequences) or love (a thing being required by guilty persons in order to relieve the other of supposed guilt) or benevolence (an acquiescence in the act of charity that is actually succumbing to the use of force, in effect using pity to control others) or any of the many, many other uses of language that pervert the meaning of reality or seek to fake it in some way. So the fit and the able and the creative and productive and successful, in other words the competent, are made to feel unremitting guilt and are given the means of assuaging it by cooperating with their persecutors. Rand calls this the "sanction of the victims."

John Galt vowed to put an end to this once and for all. And he does so for the moral reason that he is responsible for the products of his mind and the use to which they are put and will not have his creativity put to the service of evil. The mystery unfolds over nearly 700 pages as we follow the plot and become engrossed in the characterizations until John Galt vows, "I will stop the motor of the world."

Chapter 2 - The Utopia of Greed

The reader of *Atlas Shrugged* is continually faced with characterizations and settings in which the language of ordinary discourse is molded and shaped by the various available forms of double *entendre*. We do not mean by this the usual vulgar sexual innuendo. Rather the issue of the uses and abuses of language seem always to be at the front of verbal exchanges. "Greed" is one of those words bandied about to describe behaviors as diverse as making profits on sales of essential commodities and complaining about high taxes. The 1980s have been labeled in many parts of the left-leaning media and intelligentsia as a "decade of greed." It was so designated because it was the time of the massive recovery from recession and inflationary misery of the Carter years that followed upon the reduction of marginal tax rates under Ronald Reagan. It was predicted prior to these reductions in rates (not reductions in taxes paid) that actual collections would go up and the business community would have great incentives to invest and build their businesses and employ American citizens in profitable enterprises, thus advancing the collection of taxes and diminishing the need for government services. Anyone who studies the government's accounting of tax collections during that period will see that this is exactly what happened.[18] However, if one looks at deficit spending for the same period, a strange picture emerges. Deficits were in fact higher at the end of the decade than at the beginning. How so? The Congress of the US managed to piggy-back spending increases one after another on each other until they succeeded in outspending tax collections despite their record revenue collections. A segment of the political community of the nation continues to point to this phenomenon of increased deficits as a mark of the "greed" of "rich" Americans who "paid less taxes" even though they were making huge profits. The truth is that Americans of all economic levels paid more in taxes than they had ever done before and made more in profits and wages than ever before. However, those committed to redistributing the money of others to constituent groups found reason in this case to label the decade of prosperity "greedy" because people wished to retain control of their own money while others clamored to be cut in on the largesse through governmental distribution programs. This is the classic case of turning the use of language upside-down for the sake of moral posturing and the demonizing of an easy target—the "rich." The appropriate question to ask, the one that examines the premises of the charge, is this: If it is "greedy" to want to hold on to what one has productively and lawfully acquired, what is the designation of the desire to have that which another has so earned?[19]

Ayn Rand and her heroes of all stripes and levels of accomplishment proudly wear the badge given them by societal *fasciste* whose trade is in abuse of the language for the purpose of manipulation of a dense *Kultursmog* that obscures, to the unthinking, what is truly afoot.[20] If it is "greedy" to want to control one's own productivity, let them call me greedy. Midas Mulligan (Rand's "heroic" banker) legally changed his first name from Mike to Midas when he was ridiculed in the media (a reporter began to call him Midas, and it went viral) for making money in banking by supposedly turning everything he touched to gold. The secret, he said, is knowing what to touch. Hank Rearden proudly states that he expects to make a large pile of money off his metal alloy, named egotistically (so the public said) "Rearden metal," without reference to whether it is "for the

---

[18] It is not a willy-nilly tit-for-tat thing, but it does work itself out and proves that to get more of something you deregulate it and to get less of it you tax it. Phil Gramm, *Wall Street Journal*, 8/30/2012, "Reagan and Obama, A Tale of Two Recoveries," shows clearly the staggering difference between attempts to "stimulate" a recovery and simply getting government out of the way.

[19] The theme of benefiting "the needy, not the greedy" as a tax scheme was first used in the days of World War II when changes in war time tax rates were being contemplated, and New Dealers, specifically FDR, seized the opportunity to divide the electorate into these categories. See James T. Sparrow, *Warfare State: World War II Americans and the Age of Big Government* (New York: Oxford University Press, 2011), 123.

[20] The fascists of this and other ages going back to Rome manipulate state power by any means available, as Jonah Goldberg has shown us in *Liberal Fascism*, and R. E. Tyrell has kindly supplied the word (*Kultursmog*) for that dense fog of obscurity produced by such activity.

common good" or not. Dagny Taggart reacts in stupefied silence to charges that she is "conceited," though she never mentions her own abilities or achievements, and "selfish," though she has no idea what adults (for she is just a teenager) meant by the terminology and can find no one to define it for her (p. 51, Centennial Edition). Francisco D'Anconia clarifies the whole situation in a series of hammer blows, spoken to Hank Rearden (p. 454):

> You have been scorned for all those qualities of character which are your highest pride. You have been called selfish for the courage of acting on your own judgment and bearing sole responsibility for your own life. You have been called arrogant for your independent mind. You have been called cruel for your unyielding integrity. You have been called antisocial for the vision that made you venture upon undiscovered roads. You have been called ruthless for the strength and self-discipline of your drive to your purpose. You have been called greedy for the magnificence of your power to create wealth. You, who've expended an inconceivable flow of energy, have been called a parasite. You, who've created abundance where there had been nothing but wastelands and helpless, starving men before you, have been called a robber. You, who've kept them all alive, have been called an exploiter. You, the purest and most moral man among them, have been sneered at as a "vulgar materialist."

And, of course, John Galt in the book's longest speech declares where this abuse of language must end (p. 1029):

> If you search your code for guidance, for an answer to the question: "What is the good?"—the only answer you will find is "The good of others." The good is whatever others wish, whatever you feel they feel they wish, or whatever you feel they ought to feel. 'The good of others' is a magic formula that transforms anything into gold, a formula to be recited as a guarantee of moral glory and as a fumigator for any action, even the slaughter of a continent. Your standard of virtue is not an object, not an act, not a principle, but an intention. You need no proof, no reasons, no success, you need not achieve in fact the good of others—all you need to know is that your motive was the good of others, not your own. Your only definition of the good is a negation: the good is the "non-good for me."

Part of Rand's literary art is to play on this corruption of the language and use it with rapier precision to eviscerate the philosophy of popular altruism. In this spirit she names the eventual destination of the "men and women of the mind" who have been disappearing from public life throughout the book. Two-thirds of the way along we find them, "accidentally," in a place she labels with our chapter title, but which is actually known affectionately among the occupants as Galt's Gulch. It is a place where they have gone one by one to await the collapse of the system that can only treat them as pariahs and scavenge from their wealth and creativity. Once a year they gather for a month to escape the chaos of the outside world and contemplate in fraternal fellowship the future and the work they love, sharing its fruits with the others at incredibly low prices. A concert by a world-renowned composer Richard Halley is priced at a dime or a quarter, the same for a lecture by the philosopher Hugh Akston or a performance by the acclaimed actress Kay Ludlow but a course in physics by John Galt costs $10. The pricing is astronomical, though it seems to be trivial, for the only denomination of exchange is gold (silver for small change) from Midas Mulligan's bank. For the same exchange rate Dagny Taggart is hired by John Galt as a housekeeper and cook during the month of her forced stay—for she has "crashed the party" and will not be allowed out till the month is over. During that month she refuses to be a moocher on their system and works for $5, payable from Mulligan's bank in gold. As the inhabitants of the valley put it, "Only objective values count here."

One by one the characters let us know why they have gone on strike, depriving the world of the "profits" that exercising their minds would bring to the world. Those who still remain outside through each year have pledged not to exert themselves beyond the physical labor to take care of their immediate needs, refusing to let the world benefit from the overflow of the ability of their minds and what they produce. In this way they expect to "stop the motor of the world" as the world at large collapses from the weight of its own greed and envy. By this time the collapse is well under way and only two targets remain for Galt to recruit to the valley--Dagny Taggart and Hank Rearden. They remain unconvinced by Galt's argument because they cannot bear to watch what they have built over the years fall finally into the possession of those too lazy and ignorant and uproductive (besides outright evil) to even maintain the remains. During the month of her sojourn in the utopia of greed, Galt's Gulch, Hank Rearden is searching frantically for her daily in a search for her downed plane in the Rocky Mountains, even as political authorities mislead the public as to her whereabouts, reassuring them that she will return.

Each character tells us something about their own struggle to leave the world that is falling apart in favor of the valley bought by Midas Mulligan for this purpose. Hugh Akston refuses to work in a profession that denies the very existence of the thing it is supposed to specialize in knowing—the truth as perceived by the intellect of man. Mulligan states his case for "love" as the recognition one grants to "superlative values" and the reason he is on strike. Judge Narragansett quit when his ruling in a case, involving Midas Mulligan's bank (its attempt to collect a debt) and a loan coerced by government rules to be made to unqualified borrowers, was overturned in favor of the "need" of the plaintiffs rather than the rule of law. He stated the problem like this:

> Litigants obey the verdict of a tribunal solely on the premise that there is an objective rule of conduct, which they both accept. Now I saw that one man was to be bound by it, but the other was not, one was to obey a rule, the other was to assert an arbitrary wish—his need—and the law was to stand on the side of the wish. Justice was to consist of upholding the unjustifiable. I quit—because I could not have borne to hear the words "Your Honor" addressed to me by an honest man. (p. 743)

Richard Halley quit writing music for the public because, after suffering for years with no monetary success or public acknowledgement, when he finally experienced approval from the public it was as though they had no appreciation of the struggle he had endured or its reason—that he had something within himself to express for its own sake that did not need their approval to be valid and good. He says, "I saw them seeking, just as they seek to feed on Mulligan's money, to feed on those hours when I wrote my music and on that which made me write it, seeking to gnaw their way to self-esteem by extorting from me the admission that they were the goal of my music." (p. 743) Dr. Hendricks quit when medicine was put under state control to be rationed out by bureaucratic fiat and political maneuvering. "I would not place at the disposal of men whose sole qualification to rule me was their capacity to spout the fraudulent generalities that got them elected to the privilege of enforcing their wishes at the point of a gun. I would not let them dictate the purpose for which my years of study had been spent, or the conditions of my work, or my choice of patients, or the amount of my reward." (p. 744) Ellis Wyatt the oil man quit because "I didn't wish to serve as the cannibals' meal and to do the cooking, besides." (p. 744)

Kay Ludlow, renowned actress, quit and in the Gulch works in the cafeteria and is married to the pirate raider Ragnar Danneskjold (scion of a European family, who raids the shipments of governments and "looters" to return unjust income tax collections to Rand's heroes). She will no longer perform for the outside world because, "Whatever quality of human greatness I have the talent to portray—that was the quality the outer world sought to degrade. They let me play nothing but symbols of depravity, nothing but harlots, dissipation-chasers and home-wreckers, always to be beaten at the end by the little girl next door, personifying the virtue of mediocrity. They used my talent—for the defamation of itself. That was why I quit." (p. 784) An unnamed mother of two children has chosen to join her husband in the valley (for no one can force another to go on strike) because her children "represent my particular career...They're the profession I've chosen to practice, which, in spite of all the guff about motherhood, one can't practice successfully in the outer world." (p. 785) She goes on:

> I came here in order to bring up my sons as human beings. I would not surrender them to the educational systems devised to stunt a child's brain, to convince him that reason is impotent, that existence is an irrational chaos with which he's unable to deal, and thus reduce him to a state of chronic terror. You marvel at the difference between my children and those outside, Miss Taggart? Yet the cause is so simple. The cause is that here, in Galt's Gulch, there's no person who would not consider it monstrous ever to confront a child with the slightest suggestion of the irrational. (p. 785)

And another unnamed woman is the "fishmonger" of the valley. She supplies fish from the streams to Hammond's Market (Hammond himself a striker who made the finest of automobiles in the outside world). In the world of the looters she was (and still is here) a writer whom no one would publish because she believes that "when one deals with words, one deals with the mind."

All of these and others have gone on strike by vowing to refrain from doing anything beyond supporting themselves and their immediate families/dependents--until the world wakes up to its mad mania for other people's money and productivity--except what they do in the valley of Mulligan and Galt which benefits others with the same values as theirs.

29

The valley itself is powered by the motor (the greatest secret of the utopia of greed) that John Galt invented and refused to have co-opted by a vicious and covetous cadre of workers and owners at a now-defunct manufacturing plant, the Twentieth Century Motor Company. Dagny and Hank Rearden find the partially completed motor on a pile of abandoned junk in the hulking shell of the once proud facility. It is the source of an ongoing quest to find its inventor, and that quest leads to Galt's Gulch and, along the way, the cast of characters involved in the demise of the Motor Company. Along the way we meet Eugene Lawson, a man who claims he never made a profit in his entire business life as a banker (Community National Bank, inherited from what he considered to be his "greedy" forebears), whose motto was "need not greed," is now a successful political entrepreneur (he is a government regulator of sorts) who once loaned money to the owners of the Motor Company and then lost everything in the crash of his bank. Lee Hunsacker, who ran Twentieth Century into the ground and condemns the likes of Midas Mulligan for not having the altruism to loan him money without collateral or experience running a business, is now a whining charity case who lives off "friends" and resents needing to help around the house, because his "autobiography" is going to be such a success "if anyone ever gives me a chance." Midas Mulligan refused this man a loan because he violated the Mulligan standard: The man who is more evil than the one who has no pity in his heart is, "The man who uses another's pity for him as a weapon."[21]

Hunsacker makes an important point in the development of the philosophical plot, when he condemns Midas Mulligan for refusing him and his cohorts a loan:

> "Midas Mulligan was a vicious bastard with a dollar sign stamped on his heart," said Lee Hunsacker, in the fumes of the acrid stew. "My whole future depended upon a miserable half-million dollars, which was just small change to him, but when I applied for a loan, he turned me down flat—for no better reason than that I had no collateral to offer. How could I have accumulated any collateral, when nobody had ever given me a chance at anything big? Why did he lend money to others, but not to me? It was plain discrimination. He didn't even care about my feelings—he

---

[21] Centennial, 315.

said that my past record of failures disqualified me for ownership of a vegetable pushcart, let alone a motor factory. What failures? I couldn't help it if a lot of ignorant grocers refused to co-operate with me about the paper containers. By what right did he pass judgment on my ability? Why did my plans for my own future have to depend upon the arbitrary opinion of a selfish monopolist? I wasn't going to stand for that. I brought suit against him." (p. 317)

The resulting suit was the case that made Judge Narragansett quit because an emergency government rule was invoked that forced him into a decision he found unconscionable. Hunsacker goes on:

It was an economic emergency law which said that people were forbidden to discriminate for any reason whatever against any person in any matter involving his livelihood. It was used to protect day laborers and such, but it applied to me and my partners as well, didn't it? So we went to court, and we testified about the bad breaks we'd all had in the past, and I quoted Mulligan saying that I couldn't even own a vegetable pushcart, and we proved that all the members of the Amalgamated Service Corporation had no prestige, no credit, no way to make a living—and, therefore, the purchase of the motor factory was our only chance of livelihood—and, therefore, Midas Mulligan had no right to discriminate against us—and, therefore, we were entitled to demand a loan from him under the law. (pp. 317-318)

Twentieth Century Motor Company was owned by the Starnes family when its new regime of business and work was introduced. Ivy Starnes, in a pitiful hovel along the Mississippi River in Louisiana where she went to escape the crash of her family's business, explains:

My father was an evil man who cared for nothing but business. He had no time for love, only for money. My brothers and I lived on a different plane. Our aim was not to produce gadgets, but to do good. We brought a great, new plan into the factory. It was eleven years ago. We were defeated by the greed, the selfishness and the base, animal nature of men. It was the eternal conflict between spirit and matter, between soul and body. They would not renounce their bodies, which was all we asked of them. I do not remember any of those men. I do not care to remember. . . . The engineers? I believe it was they who started the hemophilia. . . . Yes, that is what I said: the hemophilia—the slow leak—the loss of blood that cannot be stopped. They ran first. They deserted us, one after another . . . Our plan? We put into practice that noble historical precept: From each according to his ability, to each according to his need. (pp. 322-323)

The plan had every person from top to bottom of the scale making the same salary. Then each year, twice a year, they would meet altogether to vote on special "needs" and assess penalties for those not deemed to have done work to the best of their ability (this is called "taxing the rich" in current vernacular, that is, punish the most productive). She continues, "Rewards were based on need, and the penalties on ability. Those whose needs were voted to be the greatest, received the most. Those who had not produced as much as the vote said they could, were fined and had to pay the fines by working overtime without pay. That was our plan. It was based on the principle of selflessness. It required men to be motivated, not by personal gain, but by love for their brothers." (p. 323)[22] The day the plan was adopted John Galt quit and vowed to stop the motor of the world. The next day the head of the experimental lab, William Hastings, quit and moved to Wyoming, eventually becoming one of the yearly visitors to Galt's Gulch after working mostly as a mechanic for a small motor company for several years.

The plan ended quickly, as Ivy Starnes laments, "In four years, a plan conceived, not by the cold calculations of the mind, but by the pure love of the heart, was brought to an end in the sordid mess of policemen, lawyers and bankruptcy proceedings." (p. 323) The Starnes family has found its end with one survivor committing suicide, one a hopeless drunk living in a flophouse, and Ivy living in bitter resentment that her fellow human beings are such louts and greed-driven animals. What we know that others did not know, while the plan was in force, is that Ivy had a secret trust fund that no one could touch, and she now lives off the pittance it ends up providing.

At the end of her quest to find someone who can work on the motor invented by the unknown genius and hero of the plot, Dagny rides in her personal rail car back toward the east mulling the disaster stalking the country. A tramp is discovered hidden in the baggage area of the car by a conductor who attempts to boot him off at a stop. Dagny intervenes and offers a meal at her own table to the tramp and engages him in conversation. He has been wandering the country working at various jobs, though he is by trade a skilled lathe operator. He is

---

[22] In a free society where one is not forced to work, if the tax rate is high enough to discourage working, they will not work beyond a certain level. That is why the scheme must be coercive in some way. This is why Ronald Reagan became sold on the Laffer Curve analysis. He knew that he had no incentive to make any more movies after a certain point of income because the tax rates confiscated his money and gave it to someone else.

clearly hopeless but unable to simply accept his fate, because as he says, "I don't think it will be any use. But there's nothing to do in the East except sit under some hedge and wait to die. I don't think I'd mind it much now, the dying. I know it would be a lot easier. Only I think that it's a sin to sit down and let your life go, without making a try for it." (p. 659) She sees in this statement a fundamental morality that jibes with her own life philosophy. Eager to know how he has been reduced to such a state, she elicits the story. Six thousand workers at Twentieth Century Motor Company voted to put in place a plan:

> Well, there was something that happened at that plant where I worked for twenty years. It was when the old man died and his heirs took over. There were three of them, two sons and a daughter, and they brought a new plan to run the factory. They let us vote on it, too, and everybody—almost everybody—voted for it. We didn't know. We thought it was good. No, that's not true, either. We thought that we were supposed to think it was good. The plan was that everybody in the factory would work according to his ability, but would be paid according to his need. (pp. 660-661)

He continued:

> None of us knew just how the plan would work, but every one of us thought that the next fellow knew it. And if anybody had doubts, he felt guilty and kept his mouth shut—because they made it sound like anyone who'd oppose the plan was a child-killer at heart and less than a human being. They told us that this plan would achieve a noble ideal. Well, how were we to know otherwise? Hadn't we heard it all our lives—from our parents and our schoolteachers and our ministers, and in every newspaper we ever read and every movie and every public speech? Hadn't we always been told that this was righteous and just? (p. 661)

As his tale continues he pours forth the saga of every attempt ever made to make such system work. If no one has a claim on his own earnings or productivity, then his only claim is his "need," his "misery, his "pain." "It took us just one meeting to discover that we had become beggars—rotten, whining, sniveling beggars all of us, because no man could claim his pay as his rightful earning, he had no rights and no earnings, his work didn't belong to him, it belonged to 'the family'. (p. 662) If superior ability means others have a claim on that ability regardless of their own incompetence or laziness or ignorance or sloppiness or uncaring joviality or sheer cussedness, what will happen to those whose ability and drive and knowledge and ambition and energy make them superior as producers? If the community cannot afford to send all children to college, then no one can send his own. If everybody can't be given a new suit, no one will. If everyone can't be provided a medical procedure, no one will. He concludes:

> What was it they'd always told us about the vicious competition of the profit system, where men had to compete for who'd do a better job than his fellows? Vicious, wasn't it? Well, they should have seen what it was like when we all had to compete with one another for who'd do the worst job possible. There's no surer way to destroy a man than to force him into a spot where he has to aim at not doing his best, where he has to struggle to do a bad job, day after day. That will finish him quicker than drink or idleness or pulling stick-ups for a living. But there was nothing else for us to do except to fake unfitness. The one accusation we feared was to be suspected of ability. Ability was like a mortgage on you that you could never pay off. (p. 663)

There is a morality here, of course. The tramp puts it in two parts. First, "We saw that we'd been given a law to live by, a moral law, they called it, which punished those who observed it—for observing it. The more you tried to live up to it, the more you suffered; the more you cheated it, the bigger reward you got. Your honesty was like a tool left at the mercy of the next man's dishonesty." (p. 665) Finally, "Love of our brothers? That's when we learned to hate our brothers for the first time in our lives. We began to hate them for every meal they swallowed, for every small pleasure they enjoyed, for one man's new shirt, for another's wife's hat, for an outing with their family, for a paint job on their house—it was taken from us, it was paid for by our privations, our denials, our hunger." (p. 665)

Just exactly what is greed? Oh well, who is John Galt?

Chapter 3 - The Guiltless Man

None of us have to settle for the best this administration offers, a dull, adventureless journey from one entitlement to the next, a government-planned life, a country where everything is free but us. –Paul Ryan (2012) commenting on "The Life of Julia" portrayed in a campaign commercial.

Eugene Lawson ended up working for the government because he excused his own failure with the idea that a small enclave of generosity and selflessness could not survive in a sea of greed and profit-making. His activities in the upper Midwest of the US were "not my fault" because he had no control over the events and people around him. He and many others like him saw that it was government that had the real power to force the masses of people in the country and the world (for that is where the novel takes us) to live together in brotherhood and love (these words are constantly used to define what the political entrepreneurs envision). For their purposes to be accomplished, the public must be made to go along with the enslavement of productive people to the will of the governing elite. This involves two primary actions: (1) The majority of people must be made dependent upon governing authorities to feed, clothe, house, entertain, and motivate them. (2) The most productive and innovative, whose abilities provide the excess capital for distribution must be made to cooperate in apparent voluntary agreement with the process. To bring this about governmental authority must turn itself to the business of writing into law and, more importantly, promulgating through "directives" more and more measures that make more and more activity criminal. In the service of this process moreover it is necessary to (1) pervert the use of language (producing irrationality) and (2) constantly maneuver the public by declaring "emergencies" that demand ever more action. A group of Rand characters works assiduously at bringing this part of the plot to a boil.

Wesley Mouch, Top Co-ordinator of the Bureau of Economic Planning and National Resources, is the prime mover in much of this activity. He got his position by posing as a lobbyist for the unsuspecting Hank Rearden. He is as

35

incompetent at planning and managing economic activity for the government as he was previously in the private sector. He came from a family that had once been quite wealthy, that is, until Wesley was appointed to manage the financial affairs by an uncle who considered him to be less dangerous because of his lack of distinctive talent or intellect. He was recommended to Rearden when he failed to produce sales in the automobile business. James Taggart (more on him later) recommended him to the Bureau of Planning in exchange for double-crossing Rearden to the benefit of Orren Boyle, Rearden's competitor in the steel industry, who had helped Taggart ruin one of his own competitors, Dan Conway. This is the landscape of the looters and moochers, all of whom pose to the public as benefactors of the "little guy." They are in Rand's terminology, "the aristocracy of pull."

There is a "head of state," generally referred to as Mr. Thompson, a kind of charismatic (not in a personal sense, but in his role as useful imagery for giving authority to laws and directives) figurehead who serves as the face of the real movers and shakers in the background. In terms of his actual skills and abilities, in Rand's words,

> He is a man who possessed the quality of never being noticed. In any group of three, his person became indistinguishable, and when seen alone it seemed to evoke a group of its own, composed of the countless persons he resembled. The country had no clear image of what he looked like: his photographs had appeared on the covers of magazines as frequently as those of his predecessors in office, but people could never be quite certain which photographs were his and which were pictures of "a mail clerk" or "a white-collar worker," accompanying articles about the daily life of the undifferentiated—except that Mr. Thompson's collars were usually wilted... Holding enormous official powers, he schemed ceaselessly to expand them, because it was expected of him by those who had pushed him into office. He had the cunning of the unintelligent and the frantic energy of the lazy. The sole secret of his rise in life was the fact that he was a product of chance and knew it and aspired to nothing else. (pp. 532-533)

Mr. Thompson is good at spitting out orders and delegating dirty work to others while he works with his advisors on speeches and ways to manipulate the attitudes of the public. Floyd Ferris is his philosophical advisor on the ways of manipulating the public. Fred Kinnan is at the table to be sure the unions of the country get what they "need" in the face of critical decisions forthcoming on who gets what out of a shrinking economic pie.

Above all, there is the arch-villain James Taggart. He is the brother of Dagny, heir to the fortune of the great Nat Taggart, builder of the Taggart Transcontinental Railroad that Dagny runs while her brother seeks favors in Washington that will loot his competitors and creditors and curry power among the circle of those doing what they do "for the good of the people as a whole." He is the secretive manipulator who thinks "making money" is about transferring it from someone else's bank account to his via government regulation and taxation. He assumes that people like his sister and Hank Rearden and Ellis Wyatt and Francisco d'Anconia will go on indefinitely providing the financing for his shenanigans because that's just what they do, "ruthlessly" creating wealth without thought of "others." He could not begin to run a railroad or build a steel mill or exploit a copper mine or finance business through banking, but he prides himself in being high-minded and public spirited in his pursuit of dividing the shrinking wealth of the nation according to "need," as long as Taggart Transcontinental is seen to be the neediest, because railroads are so essential to the "common people."

The plot is moving along throughout the meetings and negotiations of these men toward the complete control of all economic activity, eventually embodied in Directive 10-289. They have decided that the condition of the country, and actually the world, is such that a complete standstill is necessary to "catch our breath." What they mean by this is that all economic activity must be made to conform to the current status quo—no job switching, no new inventions, no price rises or cuts, same for wages, same for productivity. No one can quit a job, close a business, sell out, retire, or transfer assets. All trademarks, patents, copyrights, formulas, and inventions will be "voluntarily" surrendered to the government as "patriotic" gestures in light of the "emergency." These will then be licensed to all equally under the same name and be sold as such. All corporations and individuals will be required to spend no more and no less than they have in the immediate past accounting period. All profits, dividends, interest rates, and gifts of whatever kind will be frozen at their current rates. Naturally there are unspecified penalties and fines and consequences for failure to conform to the directive and any disputes will be settled without benefit of appeal by the Unification Board. Oh, and taxes will not be frozen because they must be flexible for any contingency they have not anticipated. This is to be the "Age of Love," where once there had been the "Age of Reason." Eugene Lawson blurts out, "Those who're big are here to serve those who aren't. If they refuse to do their moral duty, we've got to force them. This is the day of the heart. It's the weak, the meek, the sick and the humble that must be the only objects of our concern." (p. 539). As the group which has met to approve and authorize this directive, realizing that the characters we have looked at in the previous chapter will be the actual objects of this tactic, Dr. Ferris summarizes eloquently the underlying philosophy:

> There's no such thing as the intellect. A man's brain is a social product. A sum of influences that he's picked up from those around him. Nobody invents anything, he merely reflects what's floating in the social atmosphere. A genius is an intellectual scavenger and a greedy hoarder of the ideas which rightfully belong to society, from which he stole them. All thought is theft. If we do away with private fortunes, we'll have a fairer distribution of wealth. If we do away with genius, we'll have a fairer distribution of ideas. (p. 540)

But it is Fred Kinnan, the labor leader, who explodes the myth of altruistic concern that is the façade of such a monstrosity as Directive 10-289. He insists that his position controls more quantity of force than the businessmen do. He has the numbers of the people supposed to receive benefits from this arrangement, and he is determined that the outcome will favor him and his constituency above all others. Eloquently he assures them that he knows what this game is about:

> I know that I'm delivering the poor bastards into slavery, and that's all there is to it. And they know it, too. But they know that I'll have to throw them a crumb once in a while, if I want to keep my racket, while with the rest of you they wouldn't have a chance in hell. So that's why, if they've got to be under a whip, they'd rather I held it, not you—you drooling, tear-jerking, mealy-mouthed bastards of the public welfare! Do you think that outside of your college-bred pansies there's one village idiot whom you're fooling? I'm a racketeer—but I know it and my boys know it, and they know that I'll pay off. Not out of the kindness of my heart, either, and not a cent more than I can get away with, but at least they can count on that much. Sure, it makes me sick sometimes, it makes me sick right now, but it's not me who's built this kind of world—you did—so I'm

playing the game as you've set it up and I'm going to play it for as long as it lasts—which isn't going to be long for any of us! (pp. 541-542)

As the discussion proceeds, despite the evident threat from Kinnan, it is agreed that they have forgotten to prepare for closing down all research facilities, development projects, scientific foundations, and anything that might change the look of the future. They can't think about the future until everybody has received their fair share of the present—"Nobody should be allowed to waste money on the new until everybody has plenty of the old." (p. 542) Finally, voicing a growing sense of need for self-justification in the room, James Taggart seals the deal:

> "We need it. We need it, don't we?" There was no answer. "We have the right to protect our livelihood!" Nobody opposed him, but he went on with a shrill, pleading, insistence. "We'll be safe for the first time in centuries. Everybody will know his place and job, and everybody else's place and job—and we won't be at the mercy of every stray crank with a new idea. Nobody will push us out of business or steal our markets or undersell us or make us obsolete. Nobody will come to us offering some damn new gadget and putting us on the spot to decide whether we'll lose our shirt if we buy it, or whether we'll lose our shirt if we don't but somebody else does! We won't have to decide. Nobody will be permitted to decide anything. It will be decided once and for all. (p. 543)

His desperation continues in the interchange that follows as one and another respond with self-justifying pabulum. Then Taggart utters what is at the heart of this evil:

> Heroes? They've done nothing but harm, all through history. They've kept mankind running a wild race, with no breathing spell, no rest, no ease, no security. Running to catch up with them . . . always, without end . . . Just as we catch up, they're years ahead. . . . They leave us no chance . . . They've never left us a chance. . . ." His eyes were moving restlessly; he glanced at the window, but looked hastily away: he did not want to see the white obelisk [the Washington Monument] in the distance. "We're through with them. We've won. This is our age. Our world. We're going to have security—for the first time in centuries—for the first time since the beginning of the industrial revolution!" (pp. 543-544)

This sobering cry from the ring-leader forces the conversation to tail off into tit-for-tat bargaining and wrangling that finally faces the ultimate question no one wants to face: How will they get Hank Rearden to "voluntarily" give up his patent on Rearden Metal so the state can make its formula available to all parties? It must be seen as voluntary by the public or they will likely rebel at it, but the conspirators are convinced he will not do so even at the point of a gun. He has demonstrated already that he understands their need for his voluntary action, and he refuses to go along to get along. As the conversation proceeds they isolate the reason: Rearden sees himself as guiltless in a world where they have been working assiduously at making all people bear a load of guilt for something, anything that will make them pliable to the state's purposes. Dr. Ferris states the philosophical point:

> "I mean that there is no way to disarm any man," said Dr. Ferris, "except through guilt. Through that which he himself has accepted as guilt. If a man has ever stolen a dime, you can impose on him the punishment intended for a bank robber and he will take it. He'll bear any form of misery, he'll feel that he deserves no better. If there's not enough guilt in the world, we must create it. If we teach a man that it's evil to look at spring flowers and he believes us and then does it—we'll be able to do whatever we please with him. He won't defend himself. He won't feel he's worth it. He won't fight. But save us from the man who lives up to his own standards. Save us from the man of clean conscience. He's the man who'll beat us." (p. 548)

It is at this point that Taggart regains his composure and asserts his ability to "deliver" Rearden at the desired moment. We know that the plot has been developing that possibility all along. Taggart has a "secret" conspirator who has reason to want to see Rearden reduced to the un-heroic and suffering punishment. The guiltless man must be exposed. The "aristocracy of pull" will see to this business.

Chapter 4 - The Moratorium on Brains

Ayn Rand believed that the universe as we know it is benevolent. Most people consider that idea to be at least a feint toward theism. Of course, this is not true of her at all, for she was always a confirmed atheist from the time of her youth when she made the commitment to view the world from that perspective. It is arguably the reason such stalwarts of capitalism and market economics as Wm. F. Buckley and the crew assembled around the launching and nurturing of *National Review* as the banner publication of "conservatism" made the decision to virtually read her out of the conservative movement along with the likes of the John Birch Society. She is known to have chided Buckley for his unabashed Catholicism and failure to rule God out of consideration in philosophical and political thought. We would call this poor strategy, but strategy was clearly not what she was about.

By benevolence Rand meant that the universe was understandable to rational observation and by implication reality is intelligible, with the corollary that if one understands it rationally and responds in kind it is not hostile. She also clearly understood this in the Aristotelian sense; that is, that this is the nature of reality itself, not just the way we think about it or wish it to be. This is the meaning of her three section titles: Non-Contradiction, Either-or, and A is A. Stated as succinctly as possible, these three premises (or one-in-three) are the foundation of both Rand's and Aristotelian logic: The nature of reality is such that (1) something cannot be and not-be at the same time and in the same respect; (2) something either exists or does not exist at a given time and in a given respect; and (3) something is what it is at a given time and in a given respect. The "benevolence" in this is that it is so simple that any rational being can be taught its implications and no rational adult can claim exemption from its consequences. The bumper sticker motto is, "You can't fake reality," or in the words of the old TV commercial, "It's not nice to fool Mother Nature."[23] This forms a solid base from which to formulate morality for Rand. Everyone is responsible to engage in rational self interest to their own benefit and that of their fellows without the use

---

[23] For those too young to have this memory, this was a commercial for a "buttery-tasting spread" that was so close to the real thing that it angered Mother Nature.

of force for anything but self-defense or that of the innocent. Rand herself shortened this rule to "Nature to be commanded must be obeyed."[24]

The strike of the producers in *Atlas Shrugged* was brought on by the growing and stifling encroachment of a societal and political commitment to irrational impulses directed at an alleged "common good" to which all were expected to adhere regardless of their own interests or ability to see through its smarmy charade. The protagonists and antagonists we have seen so far are engaged at the highest level of the struggle to win the day—one to save the remnants of a once free and productive political economy and the other bent on establishing themselves, politicians and businessmen, as the "aristocracy of pull." The latter require a pliable public and a willing group of victims to carry out their scheme. The former are struggling to compete in an arena unfamiliar to them, in the sense that it does not come at all naturally to them to play such games. The task John Galt took for himself was to convince the producers that they could not win in a game stacked like this and must therefore deny their enemies the one thing they cannot produce on their own—the minds of their victims. The strikers gradually remove from the mix any benefit the looters and moochers might gain from the use of their minds in the conviction that one day a critical mass will be reached and society will collapse of its own mindless weight and the strikers can then return to their loved way of life.

At the center of the story is a tragic event that illustrates the corollary to this battle of the Titans. Their battle is but a symptom and result of a societal battle that has been gradually but inexorably waged through all levels of class and economics and education. The "people" for whom the aristocrats of politics and pull have been supposedly waging the war have themselves become more and more mindless, not by their own deliberate design necessarily, but by neglect and conformism and sloth and confusion and general weariness of the myriad choices incumbent upon those who would maintain their freedom. The three Aristotelian foundations of rational thought all come to bear in the fateful experience at the Winston Tunnel. Our chapter title is taken from Rand's title and is intended to

---

[24] Centennial Edition, "Essentials of Objectivism."

convey the truth that while some have gone on strike, others have been complicit, in the way we describe here, in the abdication of their own responsibility to think for themselves and find themselves caught up in the consequences of their own non-decisive decisions and irrationality. As in the case of so many of Rand's themes there is a double entendre in the title of the chapter.

The plot has proceeded to the point that the aristocracy of pull has begun to implement the Directive 10-289 mandates. Enforcement is proceeding and the bureaucracies are exploding. Taggart Transcontinental has been furnished with a substitute, Clifton Locey, for the mysteriously missing Dagny by government directive, and he is implementing the reign of mindless incompetency from the executive's office, for he is there for no other reason than political pull. James Taggart is simply along for the ride, having made his trade-offs for "delivering" Hank Rearden to the Unification Board. Taggart Transcontinental is becoming a shell of its former self as rolling stock breaks down all over the country with no one able to fix, repair, or replace the losses, since competent personnel are slipping away to who knows where, escaping the dying beast. Gradually lines are shutting down due to insufficient revenues, passengers, repairable rails, freight, and working equipment, not to mention competent employees. The one route that seems untouchable is the Comet, a coast to coast passenger train that has been the pride of TT. On the fateful day a government bigwig, Kip Chalmers, attaches his personal rail car to the Comet for a ride to the west coast for a campaign shindig that will decide his future as a politician. Along with him in the car are his mistress and several fawning sycophants whose only fraternal relationship with each other and Chalmers is fear of being left out when the game of musical chairs stops.

The critical point in the journey is an eight-mile long tunnel in the Rocky Mountains near Winston Station. Travel through this narrow passage is possible with diesel engines traveling at a rate of speed sufficient to dissipate carbon monoxide fumes that gather from exhaust. The older coal-burning engines used around the country safely are completely unsafe for this operation, so the standing order in TT has been that a spare diesel engine is always stationed at Winston in case something goes wrong with the usual engine. This permits the Comet to

43

move through no matter the breakdown and maintain its famous on-time schedule and reputation. The cold truth is that the spare engine has recently been commandeered by government operatives and moved to duty thought more politically expedient. In its place is a standard coal-burning locomotive. Naturally the Comet breaks down and the sad political dance begins, for Chalmers is not about to let anything deter him from making his campaign appearance. His methodology is the application of unabashed fear to every person and entity he can touch with hand or voice or telegram. He will not take this lying down, so to speak, and the universal fear of the actions of the Unification Board on all business and employment relationships runs rampant throughout all levels of the TT structure, up to and including the incompetents James Taggart and Mr. Locey.

Orders fly to find a diesel anywhere, get the train on schedule, insure safety, don't disappoint Mr. Chalmers, maintain the Comet's reputation, ad infinitum. Pressure builds inexorably on the station manager and his assistants and various lackeys. All of them are aware that it is suicidal to send the train through the tunnel with a coal-burning engine. No one wants to take responsibility for such an order, but they have no choice, since the Unification Board has made it illegal to quit one's job, the only apparent alternative to issuing this order. Chalmers continues to insist and the buck finally stops with an order issued to Dave Mitchum, the superintendent of the Colorado Division: "Give an engine to Mr. Chalmers at once. Send the Comet through safely and without unnecessary delay. If you are unable to perform your duties, I shall hold you responsible before the Unification Board. Clifton Locey." (p. 594) Locey makes sure he is nowhere to be found for the next several hours, and Dave Mitchum now must walk through the detritus of the moratorium on brains. "He knew that no railroad order would ever speak in such terms as giving an engine to a passenger; he knew that the thing was a show piece, he guessed what sort of show was being staged, and he felt a cold sweat at the realization of who was being framed as the goat of the show." (pp. 594-595)

Mitchum had recently gotten this job through the influence of friends with pull. He makes frantic calls to find someone somewhere who will relieve him of this consequence of being in a place without the skills or competence or courage to fix the problem. "If he held the train, they would make him the scapegoat to appease the anger of Mr. Chalmers; if he sent the train through and it did not reach the western portal of the tunnel, they would put the blame on his incompetence; they would claim that he had acted against their orders, in either case. What would he be able to prove? To whom? One could prove nothing to a tribunal that had no stated policy, no defined procedure, no rules of evidence, no binding principles—a tribunal, such as the Unification Board, that pronounced men guilty or innocent as it saw fit, with no standard of guilt or innocence." (p. 596) No one is there to absorb his date with reality. He had spent his life getting ahead and getting along in this manner and no one had taught him that just this situation is attached to this kind of bargain—"the manner in which he obtained this job, and the frame-up, were inextricable parts of a single whole." (p. 597)

After several other failed moves Mitchum decides to pass the frame along to his chief dispatcher Bill Brent. Brent is a different kind of man from Mitchum and has been sizing up the situation for several hours as it has played out. When the orders and the frame are solidly in place and Mitchum is about to exit to save his skin for the next play in the game, Brent simply says "No." In the ensuing verbal explosion he makes it plain that he will quit the job and if the sheriff wants to arrest him in the morning he'll be at his home. Brent is no philosopher. Rand paints the picture of an ordinary man caught in an unimaginable situation making a moral decision simply because he cannot evade it in his own mind and values:

> Bill Brent had learned to see, by a single glance at a few numbers on a sheet of paper, the entire trackage of a division—so he was now able to see the whole of his own life and the full price of the decision he was making. He had not fallen in love until he was past his youth; he had been thirty-six when he had found the woman he wanted. He had been engaged to her for the last four years; he had had to wait, because he had a mother to support and a widowed sister with three children. He had never been afraid of burdens, because he had known his ability to carry them, and he had never assumed an obligation unless he was certain that he could fulfill it. He had waited, he had saved his money, and now he had reached the time when he felt himself free to be happy. He was to be married in a few weeks, this coming June. (p. 601)… Bill Brent knew nothing about epistemology; but he knew that man must live by his own rational perception of reality, that he cannot act against it or escape it or find a substitute for it—and that there is no other way for him to live. (p. 602)

He is not one of Rand's Titans, or is he? Brent is the oasis of sanity and rationality who obeys the principle of highest value to Rand—he will not live in a world such as the one he finds himself entangled in. He goes to the door and calls two men as witnesses and tells Mitchum that he will do as ordered if he will give the order in front of those men. Mitchum lashes out with a crashing punch that sends him bloodied to the floor, screaming that Brent is a coward and a law-breaker. "In the slow effort of rising from the floor, through the haze of blood running into his eyes, Bill Brent looked up at the two men. He saw that they understood, but he saw the closed faces of men who did not want to understand, did not want to interfere and hated him for putting them on the spot in the name of justice. He said nothing, rose to his feet and walked out of the building." (p. 602)

Ultimately the real coward, Mitchum, foists his order upon a boy who is simply unable to fathom what is happening around him as his older fellow workers tell him it's not his job to think. He issues the order to the station agent who tells himself that things may not be as bad as they seem and the train will probably be OK. The conductor and the engineer refuse to obey the order and walk out. The station agent turns to an engineer who has recently arrived with a different train and asks if he will do the job. This engineer is drunk and in a fit of bravado tells himself and the agent he can do it. Kip Chalmers remarks to those in his car as it begins to move that fear is "the only practical way to deal with people." The train makes its way into the tunnel and never exits.

It is at this point that Rand makes the move that so often troubles unsympathetic readers. In fact, it is just at this point that Jason Lee Steorts (cited above) accuses Rand of hating her characters, of having passed from a more benevolent stage in her life to one of culpable vindictiveness. The cause for this is the following passage that we insert at length to be sure we get a fair take on it.

> It is said that catastrophes are a matter of pure chance, and there were those who would have said that the passengers of the Comet were not guilty or responsible for the thing that happened to them.

> The man in Bedroom A, Car No. 1, was a professor of sociology who taught that individual ability is of no consequence, that individual effort is futile, that an individual conscience is a useless luxury, that there is no individual mind or character or achievement, that everything is achieved collectively, and that it's masses that count, not men.

46

The man in Roomette 7, Car No. 2, was a journalist who wrote that it is proper and moral to use compulsion "for a good cause," who believed that he had the right to unleash physical force upon others—to wreck lives, throttle ambitions, strangle desires, violate convictions, to imprison, to despoil, to murder—for the sake of whatever he chose to consider as his own idea of "a good cause,"...

The woman in Roomette 10, Car No. 3, was an elderly school teacher who had spent her life turning class after class of helpless children into miserable cowards, by teaching them that the will of the majority is the only standard of good and evil...

The man in Drawing Room B, Car No. 4, was a newspaper publisher who believed that men are evil by nature and unfit for freedom, that their basic interests, if left unchecked, are to lie, to rob and to murder one another—and, therefore, men must be ruled by means of lies, robbery and murder...

The man in Bedroom H, Car No. 5, was a businessman who had acquired his business, an ore mine, with the help of a government loan, under the Equalization of Opportunity Bill.

The man in Drawing Room A, Car No. 6, was a financier who had made a fortune by buying "frozen" railroad bonds and getting his friends in Washington to "defreeze" them.

The man in Seat 5, Car No. 7, was a worker who believed that he had "a right" to a job, whether his employer wanted him or not.

The woman in Roomette 6, Car No. 8, was a lecturer who believed that, as a consumer, she had "a right" to transportation, whether the railroad people wished to provide it or not.

The man in Roomette 2, Car No. 9, was a professor of economics who advocated the abolition of private property...

The woman in Bedroom D, Car No. 10, was a mother who had put her two children to sleep in the berth above her, carefully tucking them in, protecting them from drafts and jolts; a mother whose husband held a government job enforcing directives, which she defended by saying, "I don't care, it's only the rich that they hurt. After all, I must think of my children."

The man in Roomette 3, Car No. 11, was a sniveling little neurotic who wrote cheap little plays into which, as a social message, he inserted cowardly little obscenities to the effect that all businessmen were scoundrels.

The woman in Roomette 9, Car No. 12, was a housewife who believed that she had the right to elect politicians, of whom she knew nothing, to control giant industries, of which she had no knowledge.

The man in Bedroom F, Car No. 13, was a lawyer who had said, "Me? I'll find a way to get along under any political system."

The man in Bedroom A, Car No. 14, was a professor of philosophy who taught that there is no mind—how do you know that the tunnel is dangerous?—no reality—how can you prove that the tunnel exists? —no logic—why do you claim that trains cannot move without motive power?—no principles—why should you be bound by the law of cause-and-effect?—no rights—why shouldn't you attach men to their jobs by force?—no morality—what's moral about running a railroad? —no absolutes—what difference does it make to you whether you live or die, anyway? He taught that we know nothing—why oppose the orders of your superiors?—that we can never be certain of anything—how do you know you're right?—that we must act on the expediency of the moment—you don't want to risk your job, do you?[25]

The man in Drawing Room B, Car No. 15, was an heir who had inherited his fortune, and who had kept repeating, "Why should Rearden be the only one permitted to manufacture Rearden Metal?"

The man in Bedroom A, Car No. 16, was a humanitarian who had said, "The men of ability? I do not care what or if they are made to suffer. They must be penalized in order to support the incompetent." (pp.605-606)

We cannot hope at this distance of time and space to read Ms. Rand's mind from a half-century and more of remove. What we can say is that we have met these characters before in real life and seen and heard them in operation far too many times to discount their presence and dominance among us. The remarkable thing is that Rand saw this coming and undoubtedly saw it around her. She explained the particular focus of *Atlas Shrugged* in her philosophy as creating the world that comes from the altruistic philosophy of the looters and moochers, the second-handers who live off the productivity of others and insist that it is moral to do so.[26] She made it clear that she saw this not as a neutral or benign attitude, but one of vicious predation. It is an idealized picture at each extreme to

---

[25] This is the practical world of "post-modern" thought being taught in the 21st century.

make the point in vivid Technicolor. Furthermore, using the *ad hominem* attack—suggesting as Steorts does that she has simply deteriorated in her mental and literary skills due to personal weaknesses--upon a philosophical piece of fiction does not speak to the issue she joins here—all mindlessness and irrationality has consequences, many of them absolutely tragic. Pastor Martin Niemoeller lamented his own failure to respond to Nazi persecution and murderous destruction of German national minorities during World War II by noting that he failed to stand up against Hitler's murderous tyranny upon others until it was too late to save himself, for he was now all alone. What Rand is at great pains to establish throughout this section is that the concentrated productivity of the mind is the greatest safeguard against the tragedy of life, and the failure of those who benefit from it to honor it and be duly cognizant of its value and defend it against attack is in a sense unforgivable.

The "benevolence" of the universe Rand speaks of is just as much on display in the technological revolution of a Silicon Valley as it is in the slums of Calcutta through the seemingly endless ministrations of a Mother Theresa and her order. The problem(s) in Calcutta is that it is cut off from the rational process that would actually ameliorate it for good. When that which is good is looted and diverted to the service of evil, it is truly tragic and vicious beyond understanding.

---

[26] This is in contrasting support of the portrait of the ideal man in *The Fountainhead*.

Chapter $ - The Sign of the Dollar

Francisco d'Anconia is Rand's primary foil for dealing with the multi-faceted issue of money and its meaning and uses. He is the heir of a fabulous fortune from his family's mining of copper (in Chile) and distribution throughout the world for industrial purposes and numerous other enterprises that make them perhaps the wealthiest family corporation in the world. The operation of mining and its product is essential to the great engines of the modern world such as railroads, electricity, steel mills, construction, and a myriad of other uses. It is also so secure an operation that it can go on for many years with little effort on the part of the heirs to maintain it. Many a family fortune in the real world has passed quickly into oblivion with the arrival of heirs who have no idea what it took to build the original wealth or what is required of those who would live worthy of its gift to them in the present. d'Anconia is not one of those people. As a childhood friend and early lover to Dagny Taggart (who refers to him as Frisco and he to her as Slug) he has made it his lifelong vision and ambition to push the family legacy to its greatest heights. He works in the lowest layers of the family business and at other jobs learning the meaning of work and the value of money. But, it is only under the tutelage of Hugh Akston, the philosopher, and in the friendship he shares with John Galt, beginning in university classes with Akston and Robert Stadler (the brilliant theoretical physicist), that he comes to see what the world is actually doing with his family wealth by the profusion of "people's" governments like the one in his native Chile.

For a while after leaving the Patrick Henry University d'Anconia succeeds famously as the multiplier of wealth he sought to be, so much so that anyone who wanted to see investments soar in value year by year hitched their wagon to d'Anconia copper. What's more the various governmental entities with which it dealt around the globe became more and more aware of the apparent "resource" that was theirs for the taking if they could ferret out the ways to make this pool of private wealth do the bidding and serve the purposes of the public sector. They appeared to be on the way to achieving their goals until John Galt convinced Francisco to join the strike. Having seen his own efforts diverted again and again into the coffers of others through taxation, crony-capitalism, regulation, insider trading and dealing on the markets, and outright confiscations, he comes to the conclusion that only an elaborate charade can defend his family's property and legacy from the looters and moochers. He sets out with the knowledge only of Galt and Ragnar Danneskjold (the three brilliant students of Akston and Stadler) to secure his wealth from the falling into the hands and schemes of others. As an idealized character he makes several significant speeches and is involved in several controversial moments in the plot and he has as the primary object of his speech-making the character of Hank Rearden, whom he hopes to convince to join the strike. Rearden's character, therefore, plays off against what he believes to be the dissipation inherent in the lifestyle and choices he sees in d'Anconia.

When the novel begins, d'Anconia is a world-renowned playboy, scion of one of the richest families on earth known to live and spend lavishly on "wine, women, and song" and every other debauched kind of behavior repugnant to Rand's productive characters. On the other hand, he is envied and idolized and imitated by those who see his life as the natural result of great wealth and luxury, even as publicly he is denounced as a worthless philanderer and wastrel. This is the tension built into the plot over the issue of the nature of wealth, and specifically its denomination in money, symbolized by the dollar sign, for money is treated in Rand's work for what it really is—a unit of exchange that has vastly improved the ability of mankind to turn productivity into actual wealth.[27] Through the years of barter and exchange which had no efficient monetary system that could be universally adapted to global values, wealth was painstakingly slow to accumulate and work its way through societies and classes of people. Mostly it was held by manorial and feudal arrangements of societies and governments in a system called (generally) mercantilism, which literally "filled the coffers" of monarchs and aristocracies with gold and silver and precious stones and other

---

[27] For a more detailed description and critique of Rand's philosophy of wealth and money see Steven Horowitz, "Francisco d'Anconia on Money: A Socio-Economic Analysis," in Younkins, Chap. 21.

metals.[28]   On the other hand money, the coinage and paper promise of value inherent in the dollar bill, has now become for man the measure of that which produces his survival on earth—not the concrete pieces of the exchange value they represent but the creativity and the productivity of men and women who "made" the money.   As a unit for universal trading, it has become the indispensable unit of exchange for those who would trade their own efforts for the efforts of others for their mutual benefit.[29]

James Taggart is the first to utter the words, "Money is the root of all evil."   He does it in a public declaration at his wedding reception after his marriage to Cherryl Brooks, the young and naïve but proud shop clerk whom he has taken on as a demonstration of his altruistic commitment to what he and others consider to be higher values than the mere "making of money." "Money can't buy happiness. Love will conquer any barrier and any social distance. That may be a bromide, boys, but that's how I feel," he mouths for all to hear, but we know that "love" can hardly be the word to describe what has been going on in his pursuit of Cherryl and her gratitude for his attentions. (p. 392) Lest the reader misunderstand us here, the issue is not about sex or any of the normal range of transactions that take place in a romantic fictional setting leading to marriage. This marriage is a condescending gesture on the part of Taggart, staged for public consumption and the advantage to him of appearing in the eyes of his own form of aristocracy as a benefactor of the needy and undeserving. Cherryl is only vaguely aware of this, but she is terribly confused and uncomfortable, though she is also grateful to the point of near-worship that such a powerful and wealthy man should have anything to do with a poor shop clerk like herself. Nevertheless she has her pride and has refused to trade in money for affection or anything else. The newspapers at one

---

[28] For a full discussion of the history of these issues see our forthcoming *Seeking the City*, from Kregel, Spring 2013.

[29] Rand saw the USA as the first society on earth to thoroughly incorporate this ideal into its economic fabric of life and the first to coin the phrase, "making money." She goes on to say through Francisco that Americans were the first to understand that wealth had to be created, not pillaged from others, taken by stealth, looted through taxation, passed back and forth by "redistribution," etc.

point in the society pages have denominated the relationship "the Cinderella Girl and the Democratic Businessman."

This appears to be Taggart's goal, a public persona that covers his ongoing activities, and he expects the gratitude of worship from Cherryl and the admiring public. They had met the first time after a public reception at which Taggart had been applauded as the man who built the John Galt Line for Taggart Transcontinental. Of course, he did not. His sister had forced the issue of its construction with Rearden Metal upon him and the board of directors by resigning temporarily from her position at TT and proceeding to build the line with her own capital and then to turn it over to TT at its completion. This was done to facilitate public relations with a government and public that frowned on the invention of Rearden Metal and was trying to regulate it out of existence or make it public property. Cherryl sees James as the epitome of the great railroad builder as do the unknowing public sycophants, and he takes the accolades all around after his sister has made it happen.

As Taggart makes his way through the room of the fabulous hotel where his wedding reception is being held, it becomes clear that the guest list is calculated to further the core values on which his personality is built. Others are fully aware of this, and we are privy to thoughts and conversations that show us the motives of the people present who are of two stripes—those who are able to lift Taggart to higher rungs on the ladder of pull and those who are willing to let him walk up their backs to the heights. "By the unwritten code of the day, nobody received or accepted an invitation from a man of public prominence except in token of one or the other of these motives." (p. 393) There are of course others present who have aspirations for assuming Taggart's role and more, and all of them are engaged in the rough and tumble of back door dealing that constitutes in our day "crony-capitalism." Orren Boyle is the most powerful of these at the reception. He insists on needling Taggart about the deals they have cut and the consequences involved and the future ramifications they entail. His crass way of stating what no one wishes he would state can be seen here, as he tells Taggart he had better watch himself because he (Boyle) has "friends money can't buy"—

The ones you buy aren't really worth a damn, because somebody can always offer them more, so the field's wide open to anybody and it's just like old-fashioned competition again. But if you get the goods on a man, then you've got him, then there's no higher bidder and you can count on his friendship. Well, you have friends, and so have I. You have friends I can use, and vice versa. That's all right with me—what the hell!—one's got to trade something. If we don't trade money—and the age of money is past—then we trade men." (p. 395)

The conversation that follows is down and dirty and lets both men and the reader know what kind of trading is going on in their world of legalized mayhem.

Lillian Rearden approaches and engages in a conversation about all the guests and seeks Taggart's gratitude for having given him a wedding gift—the presence of her husband at the reception. She and Taggart have had conversations before about how they might be of mutual benefit to one another. Now she pointedly lets Taggart know that any time he needs to get Hank in line she has "the goods" on him and can "deliver" him. What she inadvertently has become privy to is a deal to sell some Rearden Metal on the "black market" between Hank and a supplier of coal, Ken Dannager, in order to assure that his mills will continue to function and the railroads will continue to run. This has been necessitated by their refusal to kow-tow to the crowd of regulators whose preferred distributors of coal and steel have seen to it that Rearden and his co-conspirator are cut out of normal governmental channels. They both move on in the swirling pools of aristocratic schmoozing.

At one point Lillian confronts Dagny Taggart with listeners all around. Lillian has begged and cajoled Hank into attendance to satisfy her need to be seen with him publicly by her friends and the societal aristocracy, and Dagny has appeared reluctantly as the sister of James. Dagny and Hank have previously consummated their relationship at the time of the completion of the John Galt Line (more on this in a following chapter). Dagny is wearing a bracelet made from Rearden Metal, a bracelet which he first sought to give to his wife as a token of his loyalty and an expression to her of the pride he took in the development of his signature metal. Lillian had previously disdained it and made fun of it and him publicly in Dagny's presence, because the bracelet was not gold or silver or bejeweled and was not worthy of her or a man as wealthy as Hank Rearden.

Dagny claimed the bracelet—by trading her own very expensive necklace for it--in the midst of many expressions of horror and mortification and false embarrassment on Lillian's behalf.

By way of attempting to bait Dagny into a confrontation she boldly suggests that this evening's primary event is a mark of the power of women to make their way in the world with something tradable other than productivity and work and rational pursuits. Dagny has no interest in such a conversation, but Lillian persists as her opponent refuses to take the bait. Finally she blurts out what she means:

> Well, consider your sister-in-law, Miss Taggart. What chance did she have to rise in the world? None—by your exacting standards. She could not have made a successful career in business. She does not possess your unusual mind. Besides, men would have made it impossible for her. They would have found her too attractive. So she took advantage of the fact that men have standards which, unfortunately, are not as high as yours. She resorted to talents which, I'm sure, you despise. You have never cared to compete with us lesser women in the sole field of our ambition— in the achievement of power over men. (p. 401)

It is then that the significance of the bracelet assumes center court as Lillian attempts to exercise her "power" over Hank and Dagny with the insinuation that is not an insinuation that Dagny must return the bracelet or risk getting the reputation that she is sleeping with Lillian's husband. The entire scene turns on her supposed power over Hank and his existence as a man and the assumed wish of Dagny not to be thought of as "that kind of woman." Dagny makes it plain that Lillian's opinion and that of others is immaterial to her, and Hank insists that Lillian make apology for her display of poor taste. In this case we find one persona attempting to trade on something of value to herself that has no meaning to the two other people.

Across the room Orren Boyle listens in on a conversation involving Taggart and a group of influence peddlers and seekers who obsequiously engage in complements to the obvious superiority of his character as a "man of culture," one who "lives on a higher plain," one who is "*not* a real businessman." To them Jim responds, "We are at the dawn of a new age. We are breaking up the vicious tyranny of economic power. We will set men free of the rule of the dollar. We will release our spiritual aims from dependence on the owners of material means. We will liberate our culture from the stranglehold of the profit-chasers. We will build a society dedicated to higher ideals, and we will replace the aristocracy of money by—" "...the aristocracy of pull," another voice finishes the sentence. It is the voice of d'Anconia. (p. 404) The crowd of bejeweled and gaudily dressed aristocrats gathers around him as if transfixed by his bold and apparently unconcerned demeanor. When one woman asks him what he thinks will become of the world, he replies that it will get just what it deserves, to her horror. "Oh how cruel," she cries. "Don't you believe in the operation of the moral law," she asks. "I do," he replies. When the murmuring of the crowd grows louder, Bertram Scudder, the pundit of the aristocracy speaks to someone near him who is shocked by what she hears, "Don't let him disturb you. You know, money is the root of all evil—and he's the typical product of money." (p. 410)

The room is transfixed as Francisco refutes the evaluation of money as evil by demonstrating that it is only a tool that validates the values one already has. It is the tool of honest men who wish to deal with other honest men for the exchange of that which each values. When it is used like this its presence or absence after the exchange does not change the "wealth" of either, for they have made the exchange based on their evaluation of the other's effort and productivity and received what in their estimation is worth as much or more than the money which is the medium of exchange. It cannot make one happy but it can be used in the service of the happiness one already has. It cannot make one corrupt, but it can be used in the service of a corrupt character. It cannot make a fool wise or earn respect for the coward or the incompetent. It cannot buy the friendship or cooperation of the decent and honest, only of the corrupt and cowardly and thieving. "Money is the product of virtue, but it will not give you virtue and it will not redeem your vices. It cannot give you the unearned." But what of those who say that "the *love* of money is the root of all evil"? Here Rand engages, as she does again and again in the examination of premises:

> To love a thing is to know and love its nature. To love money is to know and love the fact that money is the creation of the best power within you, and your passkey to trade your effort for the effort of the best among men. It's the person who would sell his soul for a nickel, who is loudest in proclaiming his hatred of money—and he has good reason to hate it.

The lovers of money are willing to work for it. They know they are able to deserve it. (p. 412)

Most of the room is horrified to hear the playboy lecture them about something they all seek assiduously while denying its power and importance in their lives. Others are wondering what the wastrel is up to even being in attendance. Hank and Dagny are trying to understand what they hear and make it jibe with what they think they know of him via his public life of recent years. He makes it known that he knows most of the heavyweight players in the aristocracy of pull have been secretly buying large amounts of d'Anconia stock and that James Taggart is the largest stockholder outside the d'Anconia family. All the buying has been surreptitious in the name of phony aliases and companies. It has to be so for them because they have been party to the regulations on American companies that have made d'Anconia the only reliable source for industrial size supplies of copper left in the world. The government of Chile has been facilitating this process for years and has been raising taxes and fees on d'Anconia, justifying it because the company's stock price has skyrocketed under the explosion of outside investment, figuring a rich playboy like Francisco will either not notice or not care. But he knows, and how he cares! At the climax of the drama he cries out in fake panic to Rearden, as if he has been asking for a loan. What he has been communicating to Rearden is the fact that a series of "disasters" are about to hit d'Anconia Copper in its worldwide operations, and the people's governments that were gearing up to seize the assets will discover that the great company has wasted away under incompetent management (it will appear) so that mines have been worked in the wrong places and shipping has been bankrupted and value has been sucked dry by the apparent activities of an imbecilic playboy. When he cries out that he needs a loan before morning to prevent the crash of d'Anconia stock, the room panics and is quickly emptied except for three people left staring at one another. The implication is that they are the ones who know how to rebuild a fortune deliberately thrown away to protect it from the looters and "hitchhikers of virtue," as they have been named earlier.

Only these three--of all who have "worked" the room for favors and hidden agendas and values known to themselves and others of like mind--these three, who have seen in one another the values they hold dear, understand what d'Anconia has been saying:

> To trade by means of money is the code of the men of good will. Money rests on the axiom that every man is the owner of his mind and his effort. Money allows no power to prescribe the value of your effort except the voluntary choice of the man who is willing to trade you his effort in return. Money permits you to obtain for your goods and your labor that which they are worth to the men who buy them, but no more. Money permits no deals except those to mutual benefit by the unforced judgment of the traders. Money demands of you the recognition that men must work for their own benefit, not for their own injury, for their gain, not their loss—the recognition that they are not beasts of burden, born to carry the weight of your misery—that you must offer them values, not wounds—that the common bond among men is not the exchange of suffering, but the exchange of goods. (p. 411)

A few months later Hank Rearden is met by a man on a road in Pennsylvania that runs from his mills into the city. He is walking instead of riding because it helps to wash away the weariness of the day, which is like all the others now, where he must adhere to the administrative state and its rules to go on living. The roads are known to be unsafe because of banditry and he is carrying a gun just in case. He is met by a man of extraordinary mental powers and great courage, Ragnar Danneskjold, the pirate. Danneskjold, the third of the three great students of Hugh Akston and Dr. Stadler would have spent his life as a philosopher and teacher in another reality. Instead he is a mysterious figure preying on shipping on the high seas. Tonight his associates have blown up the illicit mills of Orren Boyle who has gotten the right through political channels to produce Rearden Metal. Danneskjold has made that impossible. He now presents Hank with a covered block of unknown nature that through the process of conversation is revealed to be solid gold, representing a down payment on an account which Ragnar has been building for him, as he has for others. The pirate has been carefully attacking only those shipments of the wealth of nations that were intended for distribution to other nations on account of their "neediness." The gold he is holding for Rearden is a growing sum that represents the income taxes he has paid over the years, just as it does for his other "clients." The bank is unnamed at this time to Rearden, but we learn it is the bank of Midas Mulligan in Galt's Gulch.

In the either-or fashion of Rand's philosophy Rearden hears the meaning of the life of the "pirate" who would be a philosopher. There are only two ways of living now before them. The life of a looter or the life of a criminal, made so by random fiat and regulation and legal maneuvering. He has chosen to fight in his own way. "There are only two modes of living left to us today: to be a looter who robs disarmed victims or to be a victim who works for the benefit of his own despoilers. I did not choose to be either." He continues, "I am merely complying with the system which my fellow men have established. If they believe that force is the proper means to deal with one another, I am giving them what they ask for. If they believe that the purpose of my life is to serve them, let them try to enforce their creed. If they believe that my mind is their property—let them come and get it." (p. 575) Finally he explains that he has taken on the role of destroying the myth of Robin Hood, the man who in popular parlance "robbed from the rich to give to the poor. Well, I'm the man who robs the poor and gives to the rich—or, to be exact, the man who robs the thieving poor and gives back to the productive rich." (p. 576) That myth, of course, has been spun out of a time when in actuality the government of Prince John was thieving from all to feather the nests of himself and his henchmen to the detriment of those who had no power against him. It has become a shibboleth of the crowd bent on using the same governmental power to steal money (and by implication productivity, that which sustains life) from one constituency to give to others who have not produced it. Robin Hood has been put in the service of the very entities that loot the wealth of the people in the name of the "common good." Danneskjold lives and risks his life for the day when that principle will be buried in the rubble of a broken civilization that tried to make it a supreme value. "If they believe that force is the proper means to deal with one another, I am giving them what they ask for. If they believe that the purpose of my life is to serve them, let them try to enforce their creed. If they believe that my mind is their property—let them come and get it." (p. 575)

Rearden cannot bring himself to take what on the surface of it is "stolen" and "criminal" in his own mind. It is this tension--a reordering of the meaning of language and values in the minds of those who have not yet "seen the light" so to speak--that remains to be worked out through the rest of the novel, for this is only halfway home to the place where neither Rearden nor Danneskjold will be denominated criminals. A place that in this story has a gold dollar sign hanging over it. But it cannot be the prevailing paradigm until Francisco's prophetic word has come to pass:

> When you see that trading is done, not by consent, but by compulsion—when you see that in order to produce, you need to obtain permission from men who produce nothing—when you see that money is flowing to those who deal, not in goods, but in favors—when you see that men get richer by graft and by pull than by work, and your laws don't protect you against them, but protect them against you—when you see corruption being rewarded and honesty becoming a self-sacrifice—you may know that your society is doomed. Money is so noble a medium that it does not compete with guns and it does not make terms with brutality. It will not permit a country to survive as half-property, half-loot. Whenever destroyers appear among men, they start by destroying money, for money is men's protection and the base of a moral existence. Destroyers seize gold and leave to its owners a counterfeit pile of paper. (p. 413)

Chapter 6 - My Brother's Keeper

*Alan Wolfe, a political science professor at Boston College, said [commenting on a study that shows "blue states" being significantly less generous in private charity than "red states"] it's wrong to link a state's religious makeup with its generosity. People in less religious states are giving in a different way by being more willing to pay higher taxes so the government can equitably distribute superior benefits, Wolfe said. And the distribution is based purely on need, rather than religious affiliation or other variables, said Wolfe, also head of the college's Boisi Center for Religion and Public Life. Wolfe said people in less religious states "view the tax money they're paying not as something that's forced upon them, but as a recognition that they belong with everyone else, that they're citizens in the common good. ... I think people here believe that when they pay their taxes, they're being altruistic." –*USA Today 8/20/2012

As d'Anconia approaches the end of his speech on money, the crowd becomes more and more restless and noisy in its indignation and a telling exchange takes place:

There were people who had listened, but now hurried away, and people who said, "It's horrible!"—"It's not true!"—"How vicious and selfish!"—saying it loudly and guardedly at once, as if wishing that their neighbors would hear them, but hoping that Francisco would not. "Señor d'Anconia," declared the woman with the earrings, "I don't agree with you!" "If you can refute a single sentence I uttered, madame, I shall hear it gratefully." "Oh, I can't answer you. I don't have any answers, my mind doesn't work that way, but I don't feel that you're right, so I know that you're wrong." "How do you know it?" "I feel it. I don't go by my head, but by my heart. You might be good at logic, but you're heartless." "Madame, when we'll see men dying of starvation around us, your heart won't be of any earthly use to save them. And I'm heartless enough to say that when you'll scream, 'but I didn't know it!'—you will not be forgiven." The woman turned away, a shudder running through the flesh of her cheeks and through the angry tremor of her voice: "Well, it's certainly a funny way to talk at a party!" (p. 415)

This moment is one of many throughout *Atlas Shrugged* that impinge upon one of the guiding justifications of the marching statism all around the characters. It is the tension between the apparent lack of "feeling" on the part of Rand's heroes and the loudly proclaimed intent of the statists and crony capitalists to be their "brother's keeper." Once again the juxtaposition of professed compassionate (feeling, pitying) involvement is met with an apparent relentless logic and rationality that defies the presence of "normal" human affection and interaction. Dagny, Hank, Francisco, Midas Mulligan, numerous striking businessmen, and ultimately John Galt are played off against James Taggart, Lillian Rearden and her mother-in-law, Philip Rearden, and various named and unnamed characters in situations where "feeling" and "logic" are made to carry varying loads of moral content depending on the purpose of those using the terminology.

Very early in the plot the theme is introduced when James Taggart is refusing to face the reality of Taggart Transcontinental's need for rails of Rearden Metal. He has been avoiding the decision and Dagny asserts that this cannot continue. In the conversation that ensues she states clearly what must and will get done and how he will do it. In frustration James whines,

> "That's all right for you, because you're lucky. Others can't do it." She replies, "Do what?" He continues, "Other people are human. They're sensitive. They can't devote their whole life to metals and engines. You're lucky—you've never had any feelings. You've never felt anything at all." As she looked at him, her dark gray eyes went slowly from astonishment to stillness, then to a strange expression that resembled a look of weariness, except that it seemed to reflect much more than the endurance of this one moment. "No, Jim," she said quietly, "I guess I've never felt anything at all." (pp. 23-24)

Not much farther along we are privy to the affairs in the family of Hank Rearden at his home where he lives with his wife and mother and brother, none of which work at any profitable enterprise or profession. Their dependency on his steel mills for their own support and survival seems only to reinforce a sense of entitlement and resentment against him. As he arrives from work on the day he has poured the first heat of Rearden Metal, he is late, and his mother reproaches him for having no feelings for the day and the problems Lillian has been going through, a day of planning a special party. All agree he has no feelings for their lives and only cares about his mills and metals and machinery and money. Lillian puts on an elaborate charade getting him to agree to be at the party to be held on a date three months hence, despite the fact he does not and cannot know what will be demanding his time then. Only after a bit of playing on his "feelings" for her is he reminded that the date is his wedding anniversary. By way of trying to explain at least a little of his distraction and lateness he pulls a bracelet made of Rearden Metal out of his pocket and gives it to Lillian as a token of the first actual object made from his signature achievement. The banter between the dependents is just barely above cynicism and is overwhelmingly sarcastic and condemnatory of his apparent conceit—his mother the worst as she states loudly that she knew he was this way when he was five years old. She accuses him of giving a gift for his own pleasure (which it is) instead of that of Lillian, who surely deserves diamonds. Later out of their presence Rearden reflects inwardly:

> What did they seek from him?—thought Rearden—what were they after? He had never asked anything of them; it was they who wished to hold him, they who pressed a claim on him—and the claim seemed to have the form of affection, but it was a form which he found harder to endure than any sort of hatred. He despised causeless affection, just as he despised unearned wealth. They professed to love him for some unknown reason and they ignored all the things for which he could wish to be loved. He wondered what response they could hope to obtain from him in such manner—if his response was what they wanted. And it was, he thought; else why those constant complaints, those unceasing accusations about his indifference? Why that chronic air of suspicion, as if they were waiting to be hurt? He had never had a desire to hurt them, but he had always felt their defensive, reproachful expectation; they seemed wounded by anything he said, it was not a matter of his words or actions, it was almost . . . almost as if they were wounded by the mere fact of his being. (p. 37)

He admits to himself that he does not "like" them, but he doesn't understand his own feelings, for he has tried to like them and have affection for them. He cannot resolve it for now. As the evening wears on he notices that his brother is showing expressions of apparent discomfort, "Philip sat in a low chair, his stomach forward, his weight on his shoulder blades, as if the miserable discomfort of his position were intended to punish the onlookers." (p. 40) Rearden's inquiry elicits comments on his normal lack of interest in Philip's life. Philip has been put through college by Hank and has yet to go to work at anything gainful. This is incomprehensible to his older brother, but Hank has been indulgent for the time being, thinking that he will surely wise up and get on about a life of work and ambition. Today, however, Philip has been engaged in trying to raise money for his favorite charity, Friends of Global Progress. He complains that he has been visiting "bloated moneybags" all day, none of which has contributed to his goal of $10,000. In the process he elaborates on the public spirited nature of his charity and the lack of "moral duty" on the part of those he has solicited. Rearden sees this as a blatant play for his sympathy without the necessity of having to ask outright, a play for money to fund projects he knows his brother disdains. We are privy to his thoughts: "It was so childishly blatant, thought Rearden, so helplessly crude: the hint and the insult, offered together. It would be so easy to squash Philip by returning the insult, he thought—by returning an insult which would be deadly because it would be true—that he could not bring himself to utter it. Surely, he thought, the poor fool knows he's at my mercy, knows he's opened himself to be hurt, so I don't have to do it, and my not doing it is my best answer, which he won't be able to miss. What sort of misery does he really live in, to get himself twisted quite so badly?" (p. 41)

In a show of goodwill he tells Philip to drop by the office tomorrow and there will be a check for the money. This offer brings on a massive conflict of the sort Rand has perfected. Philip is only mildly appreciative. Henry feels a dull ache inside that he cannot understand. Lillian remarks brightly that Henry is feeling magnanimous because it is the day of the great debut of Rearden Metal and suggests naming a national holiday after it. Hank's mother remarks, "You're a good man Henry, but not good enough." Philip then sees fit to draw out Rearden's actual lack of concern for the charity and then to defend his interest in it from purely altruistic selflessness, obviously taking pleasure in what he considers the highest virtue. Henry feels a deep loathing for the man and his moral values, "not because the words were hypocrisy, but because they were true." Philip finally requests that the money be given in cash so no one will know where it came from, since Rearden is not the kind of supporter Friends of Global Progress would want to be associated with.

The scene closes with Rearden attempting to withdraw to a window looking out at the glow of his mills, when a guest, Paul Larkin, fellow businessman, who has heard the whole thing tells him he shouldn't have given the money. Lillian chimes in climactically:

> Then Lillian's voice came, cold and gay: "But you're wrong, Paul, you're so wrong! What would happen to Henry's vanity if he didn't have us to throw alms to? What would become of his strength if he didn't have

weaker people to dominate? What would he do with himself if he didn't keep us around as dependents? It's quite all right, really, I'm not criticizing him, it's just a law of human nature." She took the metal bracelet and held it up, letting it glitter in the lamplight. "A chain," she said. "Appropriate, isn't it? It's the chain by which he holds us all in bondage." (p. 43)

The "chain" makes its next appearance at the soire Lillian had been planning three months later. Once again the room is full of aristocrats of society and business and government she has invited to impress them all with her wealth, contacts, genius for party planning, and in many ways her ability to control Henry and show him off to his evident chagrin. She wears it, in contrast to a gaudy display of excess jewelry—a trait not normally associated with her sedate style— on her bare arm, as if to make it appear especially cheap and tinny by comparison to what she can obviously afford. This will become a source of conversation and eventually of confrontation with Dagny, who offers to take the piece from her and wear it proudly (this event to which we have referred above). The significance is that Dagny knows very well what the piece of Rearden Metal actually represents in value to herself and to Hank, a factor in their personal and business relationship. It prompts a later furtive exchange of apology and regret, that is really not regret for the thing itself but for the circumstance that prompted it. Henry is torn between his mixed feelings for Lillian and for Dagny and is unable to discern the nature of his sense of rational self-condemnation for not truly siding with his wife publicly, while not feeling truly guilty of immoral behavior.

This backdoor drama plays out as the public conversations go back and forth among the various players, including Francisco d'Anconia, who has come for the express purpose of meeting and speaking to Rearden. Meanwhile, he works the room among investors in his recently nationalized mines (in Mexico, by the People's Government), playing devil's advocate to their consternation at losing their money because of the profligacy of a playboy. The mines have been worked to apparent exhaustion and due to incompetency in management and finance they are now worthless, even though hundreds of people have been paid handsome salaries to no profit. The Mexican government has gotten nothing for its trouble. Francisco is clearly mocking the investors in the room as he lauds the project for its public spirited commitment to fair wages and jobs for "those who never had a chance" and no profits turned for the owners, just concern for the workers and the "common good."

Other conversations reveal the underlying assumptions of those whose feelings for the good "of the whole" as opposed to the "selfish individual" inform their values and their politics. Dr. Pritchett, the "philosopher," muses on the nature of man: "Man's metaphysical pretensions," he said, "are preposterous. A miserable bit of protoplasm, full of ugly little concepts and mean little emotions— and it imagines itself important! Really, you know, that is the root of all the troubles in the world." (p. 131) He announces loudly that man has no standards by which to judge the good and the bad, the "ugly and mean." "The philosophers of the past were superficial," Dr. Pritchett went on. "It remained for our century to redefine the purpose of philosophy. The purpose of philosophy is not to help men find the meaning of life, but to prove to them that there isn't any." (p. 132) To a skeptical young woman he asserts, "It is this insistence of man upon meaning that makes him so difficult," said Dr. Pritchett. "Once he realizes that he is of no importance whatever in the vast scheme of the universe, that no possible significance can be attached to his activities, that it does not matter whether he lives or dies, he will become much more . . . tractable." (p. 132)

This issue of "tractability" is the essence of new legislation that has been enacted, the Equalization of Opportunity Bill, an "emergency" measure that took from certain businessmen to give to others in the name of "competition." Its supposed purpose was to help the smaller businesses against the bigger businesses in the name of the common good. It is a nightmare of inconsistencies and irrationality and crony capitalism. Pritchett defends it to a businessman:

> "Oh, that?" said Dr. Pritchett. "But I believe I made it clear that I am in favor of it, because I am in favor of a free economy. A free economy cannot exist without competition. Therefore, men must be forced to compete. Therefore, we must control men in order to force them to be free." "But, look . . . isn't that sort of a contradiction?" "Not in the higher philosophical sense. You must learn to see beyond the static definitions of old-fashioned thinking. Nothing is static in the universe. Everything is fluid." "But it stands to reason that if—" "Reason, my dear fellow, is the most naïve of all superstitions. That, at least, has been generally conceded in our age." "But I don't quite understand how we can—" "You suffer from the popular delusion of believing that things can be understood. You

do not grasp the fact that the universe is a solid contradiction." "A contradiction of what?" asked the matron. "Of itself." (pp. 132-133)

When the lady will not give up so easily he continues to "explain" to her that "the duty of thinkers is not to explain, but to demonstrate that nothing can be explained." Further, "The purpose of philosophy is not to seek knowledge, but to prove that knowledge is impossible to man." When a young woman listening in asks what is left when we prove such things, he replies, "Instinct." (p. 133)

Across the room Balph Ewbank, a writer of literature few people will buy, applies the same kind of thinking to his own field. "The literature of the past," said Balph Eubank, "was a shallow fraud. It whitewashed life in order to please the money tycoons whom it served. Morality, free will, achievement, happy endings, and man as some sort of heroic being—all that stuff is laughable to us. Our age has given depth to literature for the first time, by exposing the real essence of life." He is asked by another woman what the essence of life is and he replies "defeat and suffering." He says that happiness is "a delusion of those whose emotions are superficial." He continues by proposing an Equal Opportunity Bill for literary production that will eliminate what he regards as the lack of "literary taste" among the common people. He regards this as a great "social problem." "Our culture has sunk into a bog of materialism. Men have lost all spiritual values in their pursuit of material production and technological trickery. They're too comfortable. They will return to a nobler life if we teach them to bear privations. So we ought to place a limit upon their material greed." (p. 133) To Mort Liddy, a composer of popular musical material for commercial use, he continues, "There should be a law limiting the sale of any book to ten thousand copies. This would throw the literary market open to new talent, fresh ideas and non-commercial writing. If people were forbidden to buy a million copies of the same piece of trash, they would be forced to buy better books." (p. 134) When Liddy says that might affect the bank accounts of writers, Ewbank retorts, "So much the better. Only those whose motive is not moneymaking should be allowed to write." (p. 134)

Another young lady protests that there might be more than 10,000 people who would want to read a single book. He says it doesn't matter if more want to read it, even if, as she protests, it has a good story and is interesting to millions. His trump card is placed on the table when he avers, "Plot is a primitive vulgarity in literature." Dr. Pritchett happens to walk by as he announces this bit of wisdom and adds, "Quite so. Just as logic is a primitive vulgarity in philosophy." Liddy completes the trifecta, "Just as melody is a primitive vulgarity in music." (p. 134) Lillian Rearden floats into the group in her role as party manager and Ewbank seizes the moment to say, "Lillian, my angel, did I tell you that I'm dedicating my new novel to you?" She asks the title and he replies, *The Heart is a Milkman*, and says it's about "frustration" when she asks its subject. One of the young ladies blurts out "But, Mr. Eubank, if everything is frustration, what is there to live for?" "Brother-love," said Balph Eubank grimly. (p. 134) Such is the last gasp of an irrational world that mistakes mystical feeling for love and rational thought for unfeeling detachment.

The evening ends with Hank standing over the bed of his disinterested wife of eight years, as she prattles on about the party and the guests and trivialities and as he loathes himself for desiring her sexually. She has never responded wholeheartedly to him in that way, deliberately (it seems) silently taunting him with her lack of desire and his inability to make his mind command his body not to desire her. It is a mystery to him as he once again fights that battle while she sits in the bed filing her nails and speaking inanities to his way of thinking. Finally he conquers his inner conflict and tells her never to invite people she thinks he will like to another of her parties, to which she responds affirmatively. He leaves unable to resolve the nature of the world she inhabits and her reasons for having married him, or for that matter he her. Rand's heroic characters all deal with sexuality in this manner. They are torn by the experience of sexual desire and its disconnect from their rational existence. They refuse the tawdry dysfunction and dissolution of casual sex and the whorehouse (Rand's word). Ultimately they only find sexual satisfaction when they are united in their own complete nature, body and spirit (as Rand uses this terminology), in union with another of like mind and character. Sexuality of this kind is the expression of the values to which they are already unalterably committed. When they experience desire that is not rooted in

68

this belief in the unity of existence, they suffer, or they simply do not experience significant desire.

By way of contrast Lillian and James Taggart engage in a sexual "affair" that can only be called desultory and low beyond measure for its lack of any sense of desire or purpose other than to spite Henry. They know themselves to be merely acting out parts, and their self-loathing is evident (and they really loathe one another), but they seem to be driven to it somehow because there is some sense of obligation and expectedness about it, as if they needed to prove they could do it. Against this backdrop another tragedy occurs that brings into sharpest relief the contradictions of this chapter.

Cherryl Brooks was not married to Taggart long before she began to suspect he was not what he had seemed to her in the beginning. Through the first year of their marriage she continued to see unfold before her the real man he was, the one she really did not wish to see. She had done her best to live up to his expectations and her own aspirations as the wife of such a powerful and wealthy man. She even enlisted a paid agency to educate her in the ways of aristocratic life, ways so unlike her lowly upbringing in the slums.

> She set out to learn with the devotion, the discipline, the drive of a military cadet or a religious novice. It was the only way, she thought, of earning the height which her husband had granted her on trust, of living up to his vision of her, which it was now her duty to achieve. And, not wishing to confess it to herself, she felt also that at the end of the long task she would recapture her vision of him, that knowledge would bring back to her the man she had seen on the night of his railroad's triumph. (p. 874)

She never understood the contempt in his laughter when he found out what she was doing. Gradually, though, she began to learn the rules of the parties and affairs they attended and found herself getting more comfortable in the surroundings, comfortable enough to become a keen observer of the goings on.

The time came when she began to understand the kind of people her husband had around her. At first she assumed he had no real knowledge of their evil or was simply being polite to them. Over time it became evident to her that he might have actually been taken in by them. She began to question their character and values to Jim. She thought knowledge would remove the fog from her understanding and return the glitter to her vision of Jim, but it did not:

> Knowledge did not seem to bring her a clearer vision of Jim's world, but to make the mystery greater. She could not believe that she was supposed to feel respect for the dreary senselessness of the art shows which his friends attended, of the novels they read, of the political magazines they discussed—the art shows, where she saw the kind of drawings she had seen chalked on any pavement of her childhood's slums—the novels, that purported to prove the futility of science, industry, civilization and love, using language that her father would not have used in his drunkenest moments—the magazines, that propounded cowardly generalities, less clear and more stale than the sermons for which she had condemned the preacher of the slum mission as a mealy-mouthed old fraud. She could not believe that these things were the culture she had so reverently looked up to and so eagerly waited to discover. She felt as if she had climbed a mountain toward a jagged shape that had looked like a castle and had found it to be the crumbling ruin of a gutted warehouse. (p. 875)

The time came when she could stand it no more and began to speak her mind. "Dr. Simon Pritchett is a phony—a mean, scared old phony," she declared one evening after a party. Jim's protestations were no longer acceptable as she continued to maintain what seemed obvious to her and couldn't possibly have escaped him, in her estimation of him. Finally he tells her that he is not taken in by them at all but is engaged in a game that he expects to win where the aristocracy of pull deals with its own viciously and terminally (in the political and economic sense, but not necessarily without implications for the physical as well). The growing knowledge of the implications of this revelation haunt her life and cause continuing discussions and exchanges of anguished recriminations between them. He continues to seek her "trust" in him and she continues to try, but she knows from her own background that "honest people were never touchy about the matter of being trusted." He gets her to state her love for him and then says she must have faith in him: Love is faith, you know. Don't you see that I need it? I don't trust anyone around me, I have nothing but enemies, I am very lonely. Don't you know that I need you?" Later her torture of mind is described in a way that shouts for rational assessment of the entire question raised by the issues in this chapter:

> The thing that made her pace her room—hours later, in tortured restlessness—was that she wished desperately to believe him and did not

believe a word of it, yet knew that it was true. It was true, but not in the manner he implied, not in any manner or meaning she could ever hope to grasp. It was true that he needed her, but the nature of his need kept slipping past her every effort to define it. She did not know what he wanted of her. It was not flattery that he wanted, she had seen him listening to the obsequious compliments of liars, listening with a look of resentful inertness—almost the look of a drug addict at a dose inadequate to rouse him. But she had seen him look at her as if he were waiting for some reviving shot and, at times, as if he were begging. She had seen a flicker of life in his eyes whenever she granted him some sign of admiration—yet a burst of anger was his answer, whenever she named a reason for admiring him. He seemed to want her to consider him great, but never dare ascribe any specific content to his greatness. (p. 877)

Eventually her inner turmoil over the faith he requires of her and the truth she seeks cannot remain unresolved. She determines to go to Taggart headquarters and learn what it is Jim really does in his business. All she meets are evasive, but gradually she learns that it is Dagny and not Jim that runs Taggart Transcontinental. It is Eddie Willers who fills in all the missing pieces. "He told her the whole story, quietly, impersonally, pronouncing no verdict, expressing no opinion, never encroaching on her emotions by any sign of concern for them, speaking with the shining austerity and the awesome power of facts. He told her who ran Taggart Transcontinental. He told her the story of the John Galt Line. She listened, and what she felt was not shock, but worse: the lack of shock, as if she had always known it." (p. 880) The confrontation with Jim that follows is a microcosm of the living relationships of so many in like marriages—the guilty accused courts irrationality in the innocent accuser for the purpose of evasion of any accountability and a pretense at exoneration. Jim ultimately whines, "Have you thought of my feelings? Have you thought of what this would do to my feelings? You should have considered my feelings first! That's the first obligation of any wife—and of a woman in your position in particular! There's nothing lower and uglier than ingratitude!" Cherryl realizes what is happening, "For the flash of one instant, she grasped the unthinkable fact of a man who was guilty and knew it and was trying to escape by inducing an emotion of guilt in his victim. But she could not hold the fact inside her brain. She felt a stab of horror, the convulsion of a mind rejecting a sight that would destroy it." Near the end of the conversation Jim, still seeking that which he cannot possibly expect or demand, blurts, "There isn't any love in the world. People don't feel. I feel things. Who cares about that? All they care for is time schedules and freight loads and money." (p. 881)

Over dreary days and nights the story drags out and conversations never change. The gist of it all is that she has lost any sense of his being heroic in the realization that he is a tragic and cowardly figure trading on the effort and productivity and pull of others. The love he seeks is causeless. Even a love that finds heroic character and courageous striving attractive cannot be worthy of that which he seeks. She cannot grasp such a craving that treats her love for him, that has been dashed on the cold hard facts of his lying and cheating and double-dealing under the guise of love for his fellowman, as if it were the cheap "gold-digger" ambition of someone marrying for money. He will not accept the idea that marrying for a vision of heroic character is not the same. He denounces her, "You have the mean, scheming, calculating little soul of a shopkeeper who trades, but never gives! Love is a gift—a great, free, unconditional gift that transcends and forgives everything. What's the generosity of loving a man for his virtues? What do you give him? Nothing. It's no more than cold justice. No more than he's earned." This last seems to turn over the last card in the hand she has been dealt, and she slowly and deliberately chooses her words to let him and her own mind hear them clearly:

> All of you welfare preachers—it's not unearned money that you're after. You want handouts, but of a different kind. I'm a gold-digger of the spirit, you said, because I look for value. Then you, the welfare preachers . . . it's the spirit that you want to loot. I never thought and nobody ever told us how it could be thought of and what it would mean—the unearned in spirit. But that is what you want. You want unearned love. You want unearned admiration. You want unearned greatness. You want to be a man like Hank Rearden without the necessity of being what he is. Without the necessity of being anything. Without . . . the necessity . . . of being. (p. 884)

The final act of this year-long drama reaches its destination as Cherryl arrives home to find Jim and Lillian Rearden performing sexually in the slovenly service of disdainful treatment of the relationship they have with Henry. The confrontation between Cherryl and Jim resolves itself into his repeatedly delivering withering blasts of contempt and hatred toward her for her background and lowliness and lack of apparent "gratitude" for the way he has lifted her out of her circumstances and given her the good life. It dawns on her that the opposite of Jim's desire for an "unconditional love" is the nature of his love to her. We quote it at length so it can be seen clearly for what it is:

> "Why did you marry me?"
>
> "Because you were a cheap, helpless, preposterous little guttersnipe, who'd never have a chance at anything to equal me! Because I thought you'd love me! I thought you'd know that you had to love me!"
>
> "As you are?"
>
> "Without daring to ask what I am! Without reasons! Without putting me on the spot always to live up to reason after reason after reason, like being on some goddamn dress parade to the end of my days!"
>
> "You loved me . . . because I was worthless?"
>
> "Well, what did you think you were?"
>
> "You loved me for being rotten?"
>
> "What else did you have to offer? But you didn't have the humility to appreciate it. I wanted to be generous, I wanted to give you security—what security is there in being loved for one's virtues? The competition's wide open, like a jungle market place, a better person will always come along to beat you! But I—I was willing to love you for your flaws, for your faults and weaknesses, for your ignorance, your crudeness, your vulgarity—and that's safe, you'd have nothing to fear, nothing to hide, you could be yourself, your real, stinking, sinful, ugly self—everybody's self is a gutter—but you could hold my love, with nothing demanded of you!"
>
> "You wanted me to . . . accept your love . . . as alms?"
>
> "Did you imagine that you could earn it? Did you imagine that you could deserve to marry me, you poor little tramp? I used to buy the likes of you for the price of a meal! I wanted you to know, with every step you took, with every mouthful of caviar you swallowed, that you owed it all to me, that you had nothing and were nothing and could never hope to equal, deserve or repay!"
>
> "I . . . tried . . . to deserve it."
>
> "Of what use would you be to me, if you had?" (pp. 902-903)

She ran. She ran and ran and ran and ran in the streets of New York until there was no place to run but off the bridge into empty space.

Chapter 7 - The Clash of the Titans

A superficial reading of *Atlas Shrugged* creates the impression that the main struggle of the plot is about capitalism as opposed to socialism or some variant of it. One might also choose the individual as opposed to the collective and would come close. If you point out selfishness as a foil to altruism, you would be following the ideas of many readers and critics. On we could go with producers vs. looters and moochers, rationalism vs. irrationalism, godlessness vs. Christian concern, etc. All of these themes play their parts as the story gradually unfolds. But none of these captures the essence of the literal battle at the center of the plot—the unrelenting stalker, John Galt, who seems always to be one step ahead of Dagny Taggart in taking away just what she needs at critical moments to preserve the ever-dwindling treasure that is Taggart Transcontinental. She comes to hate first the reference to him in the question, "Who is John Galt?" and then comes to hate him as a person insofar as she can imagine him, the one she calls "the destroyer." We learn, of course, that it is no coincidence that it seems he is always a step ahead of her as she frantically does everything it takes to save her family's heritage in TT. He has deliberately targeted her for defeat in his vow to "stop the motor of the world." Yes, he loves her from afar, but he will not give in to that urge to go to her and declare his love until he has first defeated her. For amazingly enough, she is the enemy of the first order that stands between him and his overarching goal—to show the world once and for all "what is wrong" with it.

We get a growing knowledge of this "problem" through various speeches and private screenings of the thought processes of both protagonist and antagonists.[30] We are teased by the mystery of why one by one the strikers are persuaded to quit, or is it that they just grew overwhelmingly weary? Gradually we become convinced with Dagny that "the destroyer" is the key to it all. But who is he and where is he and how does he convince such people to leave their sources

---

[30] The words come from the Greek, and both have the root *agon* at the center, root for "agony," the word for struggle in the arena, such as wrestling in the ancient world. It is clear that the clash of the titans and the looters is an agony of suffering for both in different ways. One is toward the life they seek and the other is a death spiral.

of worth and happiness to disappear from societal view, never to be found? The question begins to arise especially when d'Anconia speaks with Rearden and with Dagny from time to time. Who is really the destroyer? Is Francisco the playboy who destroys his own family's wealth in a series of disastrous investments and mismanagement decisions? How can one who speaks like he does reconcile his profligate lifestyle with professions of love and devotion to the highest values? Check your premises he will say, as does Hugh Akston in the diner where Dagny eats the best burger she ever had. In this way Rand pulls us along to decipher the real story line behind the apparent window dressing.

For a while the relationship between Hank and Dagny provides solace for the two of them in a world gone mad, literally, for the irrationality of the looters is nothing short of certifiable as insanity when put up against a simple definition: Insanity is doing the same action again and again and expecting a different outcome. Or, insanity is perverting the language until up means down and down means up and believing your own perverse use of it. In a world like that, where those around you have surrendered to the perversion and insanity, it is sheer joy to be able to have a normal conversation and work with someone who does not try to convince you of the irrationality of the universe. Such is the relationship that Rearden and Dagny have, which also leads to their becoming lovers at the completion of the building of the John Galt Line. But even this joy is to be short-lived, as Francisco predicted when she named the line after the non-man of the universal question in the novel. Francisco knows what the question means and to whom it refers and he warns Dagny about using the name. She defies whoever it is to come and take the line from her. Francisco assures her he, John Galt, will do just that. Meanwhile, it is she and Rearden who seem to stand alone against the encroaching darkness, as lights are going out all over the world's cities, rail traffic is slowing and diminishing in volume, mining and steel making are being reduced to trivial production of consumer goods instead of industrial uses, gangs of looters and marauders roam the countryside looking for victims, ghost trains are abandoned in the expanses between cities, and the world is gradually coming to an economic standstill.

Still she cannot quit and damns those who have and in so doing have left her to fight alone it seems. In it all the mystery motor the two found at Twentieth Century Motor Company is in the hands of a young scientist, Quentin Daniels, who is working at a closed college in Utah as a janitor so he can have free use of the lab and its equipment. He has been sending reports and she has been sending him checks. Eventually, she gets a letter from him that he is quitting. His reasons are worth reading at length:

Dear Miss Taggart:
I have fought it out for three weeks, I did not want to do it, I know how this will hit you and I know every argument you could offer me, because I have used them all against myself—but this is to tell you that I am quitting. I cannot work under the terms of Directive 10-289—though not for the reasons its perpetrators intended. I know that their abolition of all scientific research does not mean a damn to you or me, and that you would want me to continue. But I have to quit, because I do not wish to succeed any longer. I do not wish to work in a world that regards me as a slave. I do not wish to be of any value to people.
If I succeeded in rebuilding the motor, I would not let you place it in their service. I would not take it upon my conscience that anything produced by my mind should be used to bring them comfort. I know that if we succeed, they will be only too eager to expropriate the motor. And for the sake of that prospect, we have to accept the position of criminals, you and I, and live under the threat of being arrested at any moment at their whim. And this is the thing that I cannot take, even were I able to take all the rest: that in order to give them an inestimable benefit, we should be made martyrs to the men who, but for us, could not have conceived of it. I might have forgiven the rest, but when I think of this, I say: May they be damned, I will see them all die of starvation, myself included, rather than forgive them for this or permit it!
To tell you the full truth, I want to succeed, to solve the secret of the motor, as much as ever. So I shall continue to work on it for my own sole pleasure and for as long as I last. But if I solve it, it will remain my private secret. I will not release it for any commercial use. Therefore, I cannot take your money any longer. Commercialism is supposed to be despicable, so all those people should truly approve of my decision. And I—I'm tired of helping those who despise me.
I don't know how long I will last or what I will do in the future. For the moment, I intend to remain in my job at this Institute. But if any of its trustees or receivers should remind me that I am now legally forbidden to cease being a janitor, I will quit. You had given me my greatest chance and if I am now giving you a painful blow, perhaps I should ask you to forgive me. I think that you love your work—as much as I loved mine, so you will know that my decision was not easy to make, but that I had to make it. It is a strange feeling—writing this letter. I do not intend to die,

but I am giving up the world and this feels like the letter of a suicide. So I want to say that of all the people I have known, you are the only person I regret leaving behind. (p. 645)

Dagny's response to this letter is what gets her eventually into Galt's Gulch, for she calls Daniels and urgently insists that he wait until she has gotten there and had time to talk to him. Meanwhile the destroyer arrives and convinces Daniels to go with him and the reason he does is two-fold. The intruder walks to the blackboard and writes out a formula that Daniels will recognize as the key to the workings of the motor. The second is his validation of the things we see in the letter above. The excitement of the moment makes him forget that he had promised to wait for Dagny and he and the destroyer are just taking off enroute to Galt's Gulch when she arrives in her plane. She follows them until they disappear and then eventually crash lands with the consequences we have noted above.

At last she meets the destroyer and is challenged with his insistence that she is the problem still left in the world. "Did you know who I was, when you saw me for the first time?" "Oh yes. My worst enemy but one." "What?" She had not expected it; she added, more quietly, "Who's the worst one?" "Dr. Robert Stadler." "Did you have me classified with him?" "No. He's my conscious enemy. He's the man who sold his soul. We don't intend to reclaim him. You—you were one of us. I knew it, long before I saw you. I knew also that you would be the last to join us and the hardest one to defeat." (p. 778) Later he tells her "Every man that your railroad needed and lost in the past ten years," he said, "it was I who made you lose him...I have pulled every girder from under Taggart Transcontinental and, if you choose to go back, I will see it collapse upon your head." (p. 780) Over the weeks of her stay with the strikers she hears from one and another and another again and again that what has held these once in chains has been resolved for them. Their very determination to follow their own understanding of virtue and goodness with total dedication was being used against them to make them support a world that despised them and disdained their achievements and taxed and regulated them for the benefit of the lazy and indolent and dissipated and villainous in the name of love and brotherhood and compassion and the common good and the benefit of the whole and a thousand other clichés. These victims had now decided no longer to be victimized for the future of a world that could not live without them and which they themselves despised for its dedication to irrationality and phony altruism. That world was now collapsing under its own weight and they were doing what they could to hasten its demise. Her maintenance of the lifeblood of rail transportation was one of the last links to civilization left. That made her an enemy of the strikers themselves, but it also made her an enemy of her own values. This final step, which they had all taken, was her most formidable hurdle. She explains on the last day before departing, "If you want to know the one reason that's taking me back, I'll tell you: I cannot bring myself to abandon to destruction all the greatness of the world, all that which was mine and yours, which was made by us and is still ours by right—because I cannot believe that men can refuse to see, that they can remain blind and deaf to us forever, when the truth is ours and their lives depend on accepting it. They still love their lives—and that is the uncorrupted remnant of their minds. So long as men desire to live, I cannot lose my battle." The response is chilling: "Do they?" said Hugh Akston softly. "Do they desire it?" (p. 807) Another "check your premises" moment!

The principle in operation here, a virtuous person refusing to give up on a world that is bound to take her life-blood from her an ounce at a time while damning her right to live from her own efforts and productivity, is called "the sanction of the victim." John Galt clarifies it in his famous speech:

> Then I saw what was wrong with the world, I saw what destroyed men and nations, and where the battle for life had to be fought. I saw that the enemy was an inverted morality—and that my sanction was its only power. I saw that evil was impotent—that evil was the irrational, the blind, the anti-real—and that the only weapon of its triumph was the willingness of the good to serve it. Just as the parasites around me were proclaiming their helpless dependence on my mind and were expecting me voluntarily to accept a slavery they had no power to enforce, just as they were counting on my self-immolation to provide them with the means of their plan—so throughout the world and throughout men's history, in every version and form, from the extortions of loafing relatives to the atrocities of collective countries, it is the good, the able, the men of reason, who act as their own destroyers, who transfuse to evil the blood of their virtue and let evil transmit to them the poison of destruction, thus gaining for evil the power of survival, and for their own values—the impotence of death. I saw that there comes a point, in the defeat of any man of virtue, when his own consent is needed for evil to win—and that no manner of injury done to him by others can succeed if he chooses to

withhold his consent. I saw that I could put an end to your outrages by pronouncing a single word in my mind. I pronounced it. The word was "No." (p. 1048)

From this moment, the time when Twentieth Century Motor Company put in place its famous "plan" for implementing "from each according to his ability to each according to his need," Galt vowed to live a life that would not produce a profit or benefit to another other than his own survival (and for others, their dependents) and would pursue and persuade others to do the same until the motor of the world stopped. Dagny was clearly one of those who lived as the others had, to find happiness in productive living and let the extras fall where they might to the benefit of others. She did not live off the effort of others, and she applauded the achievement of those whose talents and abilities brought additional wealth to her life. She, therefore, was a target for the destroyer until she joined the strikers in understanding what must be done, but only of her own volition and without pitying the others or thinking she must do it for them.

On the other hand, Dr. Stadler was a true enemy for whom their was no hope, for he had joined the other side. He was a betrayer who had once held to the same values as Galt and was his teacher. But he had joined the looters by making the Science Institute at Patrick Henry University an adjunct of the state that was now named the State Science Institute. He claimed it was for the common good and the benefit of the people as a whole. He prided himself in not being part of the pursuit of profits. He had cut out certain privileges for himself in pursuit of his own pet projects that he claimed would benefit all the people and not just some greedy businessman after a profit. Of course, he justified taking state money and making its products a possession of the state by claiming it was all for good and altruistic purposes, not his own benefit. The truth was, however, he had become a servant of the state whose work was being used to produce instruments of destruction and torture that would be put in service to those seeking the coercion of men and women deemed to be enemies of the states social policies. These included especially businessmen who were recalcitrant to the new emergency rules, but they had already been demonstrated in their power to terrorize the masses with their destructive capabilities. Eventually John Galt will become their primary object lesson. Stadler cannot be reclaimed, but Dagny is an "enemy" that can be "beaten" in a fair fight.

Such is the confusion of values, of virtues and vices, in a world given to irrationality by its rulers. One must fight the battle one has been given to restore sanity. Hugh Akston went on strike rather than stay in the employ of an institution that sanctioned such a world in its philosophy departments: "When thinkers accept those who deny the existence of thinking, as fellow thinkers of a different school of thought—it is they who achieve the destruction of the mind. They grant the enemy's basic premise, thus granting the sanction of reason to formal dementia. A basic premise is an absolute that permits no co-operation with its antithesis and tolerates no tolerance." (pp. 741-742) He refused to grant an irrational basic premise for conversation. If he had, he would have become part of the problem. He and Galt are making a clear distinction between the betrayer and the unwitting abettor of one's own sufferings. Rand's characters all grant that it is possible to be wrong in one's judgments and conclusions and to require examination of the premises of one's actions, but it is unforgivable (unless one changes) to refuse to think (in favor of "feeling") or to persist in patently irrational patterns of thought based on palpably wrong or pernicious premises. There are "enemies" and there are enemies.

There are also comrades in arms and fellow-laborers and those who are in the vanguard of aspiration to higher attainment and ideals and those who would learn from those who have moved on ahead. Otherwise there would be no reason for a destroyer and nothing to carry the plot. The idealized and almost mythical "Titans" are there to clarify the issues for those interested in Rand's philosophical ideals. John Galt is the ultimate teacher, surpassing even his own teacher. But others are clearly teachers of a sort along the way. Dagny is a constant influence on Eddie Willers, who has loved her from their childhood and is the only person she will trust fully to implement her directives as chief of operations. Willers is also influenced by Galt without realizing what is going on. He is the kind of man the most creative visualize as benefiting from their work. We see this in the sequence between d'Anconia and Rearden when he is about to go on trial for making a deal to sell some of his Metal outside the government's rules. Francisco

80

asks him what kind of men he wanted to ride on his rails and have better lives. Of course the men who are being taken out of the world by Galt are mentioned, but then he asks, "Did you want to see it used by men who could not equal the power of your mind, but who would equal your moral integrity—men such as Eddie Willers—who could never invent your Metal, but who would do their best, work as hard as you did, live by their own effort, and—riding on your rail—give a moment's silent thanks to the man who gave them more than they could give him?" "Yes," said Rearden gently. (p. 453)

Much of the novel is seen through the eyes of this common man, though he is not recruited to go on strike. At the end of the collapse of the TT system he is in charge of the last hours of the final run of the Comet. The train has been abandoned in the wasteland between cities, and he cannot stop the inexorable. He has no resources left but his sheer will to survive and not let the Comet die:

> He was pulling at coils of wire, he was linking them and tearing them apart—while the sudden sense of sunrays and pine trees kept pulling at the corners of his mind. Dagny!—he heard himself crying soundlessly—Dagny, in the name of the best within us! . . . He was jerking at futile levers and at a throttle that had nothing to move. . . . Dagny!—he was crying to a twelve-year-old girl in a sunlit clearing of the woods—in the name of the best within us, I must now start this train! . . . Dagny, that is what it was . . . and you knew it, then, but I didn't . . . you knew it when you turned to look at the rails. . . . I said, "not business or earning a living" . . . but, Dagny, business and earning a living and that in man which makes it possible—that is the best within us, that was the thing to defend . . . in the name of saving it, Dagny, I must now start this train . . . (p. 1166)

The pathos of the scene is overwhelming, but it represents the essence of the titanic struggle that has gone on for almost 1200 pages. It is most telling in its juxtaposition to the burst of sound in the next paragraph, the sound of Richard Halley's Concerto of triumph in the Valley of the heroes, for the death of the Comet is the signal for the rise of a new world from the ashes of the old. It should not be lost on us that the collapse of Eddie Willers does not happen until the men of the mind have been fully extracted from the chaos created by those who believed it possible to build a livable world without them. It is the Eddie Willerses of the world who then suffer the most, for they do not have the over-the-top abilities to actually change the context within which all of us live.

Across the country a bit earlier in the story another small story within the story has reached a climax. Washington had sent a spy to tag along with Hank Rearden about a fourth of the way through the book. Rearden refers to him as "Non-Absolute" and the "Wet Nurse" in various settings, having surmised the mission on which the young man has been sent. He is supposed to oversee compliance with the web of directives designed to hamstring business and Rearden in particular. Along the way he begins to warm up to his relationship with his boss and seeks to instruct him on the ways of Washington politics and the means of gaining favors. His justification is that nothing is absolute and everything is relative anyway, so why not take advantage of the situation? The steel man growls to Mr. Non-Absolute, just try to pour a heat of steel or build a mill without absolutes. In time there is a grudging respect for Rearden growing in the young man, and he overlooks a back door deal Hank makes with Ken Danagger. Rearden assumes he is saving the information to play against him at some ideal time of his own choosing. He questions him about it and finds the boy is losing his confidence in the ways of Washington.

The Wet Nurse becomes an admirer of the process of steel making and the character he sees in Rearden. When Rearden finds him hanging out on a holiday in the offices and out watching the process of pouring steel, he asks him what he is doing there on a holiday. He finds out the boy has no real family and once studied to be a metallurgist before he found his job in Washington. The conversation is wistful for both characters as they explore in their minds what it would have been like for them to be father and son. One day he asks Rearden, "What's a moral premise?" This elicits the reply, "What you're going to have a lot of trouble with." The issue heats up when James Taggart arranges to extort the patent for Rearden Metal away from Henry and make it the property of the state and Orren Boyle in particular. The Wet Nurse has found out about the plot and is outraged. The exchange between the two is telling:

> "Mr. Rearden," he said, "I wanted to tell you that if you want to pour ten times the quota of Rearden Metal or steel or pig iron or anything, and bootleg it all over the place to anybody at any price—I wanted to tell you to go ahead. I'll fix it up. I'll juggle the books, I'll fake the reports, I'll get phony witnesses, I'll forge affidavits, I'll commit perjury—so you don't have to worry, there won't be any trouble!" "Now why do you want

to do that?" asked Rearden, smiling, but his smile vanished when he heard the boy answer earnestly: "Because I want, for once, to do something moral." "That's not the way to be moral—" Rearden started, and stopped abruptly, realizing that it was the way, the only way left, realizing through how many twists of intellectual corruption upon corruption this boy had to struggle toward his momentous discovery. "I guess that's not the word," the boy said sheepishly. "I know it's a stuffy, old-fashioned word: That's not what I meant. I meant—" It was a sudden, desperate cry of incredulous anger... (pp. 555-556)

Still later on the Non-Absolute asks for a job, as he realizes the dirty business he is employed to carry out and simply cannot live with it any longer:

"I want to quit what I'm doing and go to work. I mean, real work—in steel-making, like I thought I'd started to, once. I want to earn my keep. I'm tired of being a bedbug."

After Rearden shows his shock and disbelief, the boy continues,

"I mean it, Mr. Rearden. And I know what the word means and it's the right word. I'm tired of being paid, with your money, to do nothing except make it impossible for you to make any money at all. I know that anyone who works today is only a sucker for bastards like me, but . . . well, God damn it, I'd rather be a sucker, if that's all there's left to be!" (p. 934)

The conversion is complete!

Ultimately the government and its henchman among unionists cannot be stopped. The mills are invaded by union-inspired and hired goon squads, and the young man makes a vain attempt to stop the violent takeover. They shoot him and leave him for dead. When Rearden arrives at the scene he finds the boy at the top of a slag heap wounded and dying with bloodied hands and face and knees. The dying conversation reveals that the whole thing has been staged to justify taking over the steel industry. The boy has had all he will take and staked his life on trying to stop it and get Rearden there before it was too late. Rearden realizes from the conversation that he was dropped at the bottom of the huge heap and has clawed his way to the top to try to get word to him. As he is dying he realizes he has accomplished this last act of heroism and asks Rearden, "Mr. Rearden, is this how it feels to . . . to want something very much . . . very desperately much . . . and to make it?" Rearden manages to answer yes. Hank attempts to get him to be calm and let him take him to the hospital, but the boy knows he is dying. As Rearden relents and lets him lie undisturbed, he says,

> "I won't make it, Mr. Rearden . . . No use fooling myself . . . I know I'm through." Then, as if by some dim recoil against self-pity, he added, reciting a memorized lesson, his voice a desperate attempt at his old, cynical, intellectual tone, "What does it matter, Mr. Rearden? . . . Man is only a collection of . . . conditioned chemicals . . . and a man's dying doesn't make . . . any more difference than an animal's." "You know better than that." "Yes," he whispered. "Yes, I guess I do." (p. 991)

As the struggle between life and death play out, the boy, who in another reality might have been his son, puts the exclamation point to much of Rand's bottom line philosophy:

> "I know . . . it's crap, all those things they taught us . . . all of it, everything they said . . . about living or . . . or dying . . . Dying . . . it wouldn't make any difference to chemicals, but—" he stopped, and all of his desperate protest was only in the intensity of his voice dropping lower to say, "—but it does, to me . . . And . . . and, I guess, it makes a difference to an animal, too . . . But they said there are no values . . . only social customs . . . No values!...I'd like to live, Mr. Rearden. God, how I'd like to!" His voice was passionately quiet. "Not because I'm dying . . . but because I've just discovered it tonight, what it means, really to be alive . . . And . . . it's funny . . . do you know when I discovered it? . . . In the office . . . when I stuck my neck out . . . when I told the bastards to go to hell . . . There's . . . there's so many things I wish I'd known sooner . . . But . . . well, it's no use crying over spilled milk."

A few moments later Rearden attempts to calm him and steel his courage for an attempt to move to the hospital being carried by Rearden himself. In the exchange he calls the boy Tony.

> He saw a sudden flicker in the boy's face, an attempt at his old, bright, impudent grin. "Not 'Non-Absolute' any more?" "No, not any more. You're a full absolute now, and you know it." "Yes. I know several of them, now. There's one"—he pointed at the wound in his chest—"that's an absolute, isn't it? And"—he went on speaking while Rearden was lifting him from the ground by imperceptible seconds and inches, speaking as if the trembling intensity of his words were serving as an anesthetic against the pain—"and men can't live . . . if rotten bastards . . . like the ones in Washington . . . get away with things like . . . like the one they're doing tonight . . . if everything becomes a stinking fake . . . and nothing is real . . . and nobody is anybody . . . men can't live that way . . . that's an absolute, isn't it?" "Yes, Tony, that's an absolute." (pp. 992-993)

84

The mills are eventually "saved" by the organization of his own tested men and the leadership of Francisco d'Anconia who has been working secretly for him as a foreman, but really being his body guard. But the realities of the experience have made him ready for the *coup de gras* by his "savior." He has had enough of the guilt that had kept him working in slavery for others of unknown and known description, whose only response was to disdain his efforts and reach out a hand for more.

> He knew that the meaning of his mills had ceased to exist, and the fullness of the knowledge left no room for the pain of regretting an illusion. He had seen, in a final image, the soul and essence of his enemies: the mindless face of the thug with the club. It was not the face itself that made him draw back in horror, but the professors, the philosophers, the moralists, the mystics who had released that face upon the world...If it's true, he thought, that there are avengers who are working for the deliverance of men like me, let them see me now, let them tell me their secret, let them claim me, let them—"Come in!" he said aloud, in answer to the knock on his door. (pp. 997-998)

Chapter 8 - Who Is John Galt?

Let Dagny Taggart answer that question:

> You—she thought—whoever you are, whom I have always loved and never found, you whom I expected to see at the end of the rails beyond the horizon, you whose presence I had always felt in the streets of the city and whose world I had wanted to build, it is my love for you that had kept me moving, my love and my hope to reach you and my wish to be worthy of you on the day when I would stand before you face to face. Now I know that I shall never find you—that it is not to be reached or lived—but what is left of my life is still yours, and I will go on in your name, even though it is a name I'll never learn, I will go on serving you, even though I'm never to win, I will go on, to be worthy of you on the day when I would have met you, even though I won't. . . . She had never accepted hopelessness, but she stood at the window and, addressed to the shape of a fogbound city, it was her self-dedication to unrequited love. (p. 634)

She thinks these thoughts even as she realizes it appears to be a hopeless quest to continue running Taggart Transcontinental in the face of the approaching national and international catastrophes. She has just admitted to Hank Rearden, who has signed his signature metal over to the government because of the extortion of James Taggart,

> Hank, I don't think they care whether there's a train or a blast furnace left on earth. We do. They're holding us by our love of it, and we'll go on paying so long as there's still one chance left to keep one single wheel alive and moving in token of human intelligence. We'll go on holding it afloat, like our drowning child, and when the flood swallows it, we'll go down with the last wheel and the last syllogism. I know what we're paying, but—price is no object any longer. (p. 632)

She has not yet met John Galt, and she is still committed to her relationship to Rearden. She has returned from an absence during which she has weighed the price of continuing her own battle. The catalyst for her return is the tunnel disaster we have related above. Her statement to Hank is the essence of the truth Galt has been impressing upon those he takes from her at every turn. It is clear she knows the price she is paying and is bound in her own mind to continue doing so. In the loneliness of her apartment she looks out at the lights and streets of New York and reflects on her passion for work and achievement and the man she knows she has been seeking all her life. A ring of the doorbell reveals the presence of her childhood and youthful friend and lover, Francisco. He has come

in the hope she has arrived at the conclusion he and Galt and others have seen.
His disappointment is painful as the conversation proceeds:

> "If Taggart Transcontinental is to perish with the looters, then so am I."
> He did not take his eyes off her face and he did not answer. She added
> dispassionately, "I thought I could live without it. I can't. I'll never try it
> again. Francisco, do you remember?—we both believed, when we started,
> that the only sin on earth was to do things badly. I still believe it." The
> first note of life shuddered in her voice. "I can't stand by and watch what
> they did at that tunnel. I can't accept what they're all accepting—
> Francisco, it's the thing we thought so monstrous, you and I!—the belief
> that disasters are one's natural fate, to be borne, not fought. I can't accept
> submission. I can't accept helplessness. I can't accept renunciation. So
> long as there's a railroad left to run, I'll run it." "In order to maintain the
> looters' world?" "In order to maintain the last strip of mine."
> "Dagny," he said slowly, "I know why one loves one's work. I know
> what it means to you, the job of running trains. But you would not run
> them if they were empty. Dagny, what is it you see when you think of a
> moving train?"
> She glanced at the city. "The life of a man of ability who might have
> perished in that catastrophe, but will escape the next one, which I'll
> prevent—a man who has an intransigent mind and an unlimited ambition,
> and is in love with his own life . . . the kind of man who is what we were
> when we started, you and I. You gave him up. I can't."
> "Do you think that you can still serve him—that kind of man—by
> running the railroad?" "Yes."
> "All right, Dagny. I won't try to stop you. So long as you still think that,
> nothing can stop you, or should. You will stop on the day when you'll
> discover that your work has been placed in the service, not of that man's
> life, but of his destruction." (p. 635)

The conversation proceeds as they discuss whether this man exists at all.
Francisco assures her he does, without naming him. He then describes what kind
of man he is in these powerful words:

> You know, Dagny, we were taught that some things belong to God and
> others to Caesar. Perhaps their God would permit it. But the man you say
> we're serving—he does not permit it. He permits no divided allegiance,
> no war between your mind and your body, no gulf between your values
> and your actions, no tributes to Caesar. He permits no Caesars." (p. 636)

This statement elicits from Dagny an assurance that if she ever comes to see what
Francisco is trying to explain, she will beg for forgiveness on her knees. He
assures her she will beg for forgiveness, but not on her knees. He then makes the
statement of his purpose crystal clear in the language we have seen in the last
chapter:

Until then, Dagny, remember that we're enemies. I didn't want to tell you this, but you're the first person who almost stepped into heaven and came back to earth. You've glimpsed too much, so you have to know this clearly. It's you that I'm fighting, not your brother James or Wesley Mouch. It's you that I have to defeat. I am out to end all the things that are most precious to you right now. While you'll struggle to save Taggart Transcontinental, I will be working to destroy it. Don't ever ask me for help or money. You know my reasons. Now you may hate me—as, from your stand, you should. (p. 636)

Her response is a cry and his answer is an exclamation point to his disappointment and her continued quest:

"Francisco!" she cried, in desperate defense of him against herself. "How can you do what you're doing?" "By the grace of my love"—for you, said his eyes—"for the man," said his voice, "who did not perish in your catastrophe and who will never perish." (p. 637)

This is who John Galt is—the single vision of an ideal man in the mind of Dagny Taggart, who is clearly standing in for Ayn Rand herself. In the previous chapter we saw that he is the enemy of all that Dagny holds dear in her world, and that he has vowed to stop that world in its tracks. In the process he must defeat her, but that requires his remaining somewhere in her world. We discover through her stay in Galt's Gulch that he is actually her secret lover, a love that has never been consummated sexually, and is not during her stay. But his defense of returning to the outside world betrays his clear intention to win her to himself completely, and that he is willing to pay any price to do so. This is clearly what the literary world knows as "romantic" tension, though it is just as clearly in service of the philosophical ends in view. The sexual and "romantic" issues will not be settled without resolving the main conflict that takes 1200 pages to reach its denouement. Nevertheless, it is inescapable that the tension between the two is that between the sexes which must reach its consummation or die in rejection. Dagny as "enemy" is never defeated by Galt's persuasion or argumentation. She is ultimately defeated by her inability to live without his presence in her life while she knows he is somewhere near at hand. When she discovers that he has been working for her as a track laborer for several years, and she manages to find his local address, she cannot resist going to him, even though he has warned her that she will be used by the authorities to find and get at him. He "wins" when she is driven to find him, but the state's thugs are right behind. She must engage in an elaborate betrayal charade in order to convince them that Galt is her enemy and that she has deliberately led them to him. In the brief interim between her arrival at his door and the arrival of her followers he explains that he is willing to suffer anything at their hands, but he is unwilling to endure what they will do to her if they believe she is important to him, especially if they know of their love for one another.

Francisco's prophecy comes true as she sees him taken away at their mercy. Now she sees that her very presence has become the cause of his apparent defeat and eventual torture and possible death. The last sequences of the novel show how a state apparatus that is run by men who do not know how to actually produce and multiply wealth, only to confiscate and distribute it, requires some form of popular approval to survive—it must be sanctioned in some way by its victims. Their ridiculous mission in Galt's case is to force him to take command and rule, thus rescuing their bacon. He simply refuses every persuasion, every trick, every inducement—he clearly does not live his life for the sake of money or position or pleasure--until in exasperation threats begin to come, and finally they resort to a torture chamber.[31] The device they use is the one produced from the scientific research of Robert Stadler, the man who believed in the purity of science and disdained its use for something as trivial as a motor, even one like Galt has invented, what we might call the ultimate "green machine." By converting static electricity to power, it promises unlimited power for any use without diminishing resources or adding to pollution (issues important to us, but not to Rand in her day). The torture machine, nicknamed the Ferris Persuader, is designed to induce varying degrees of pain electrically to all parts of the body simultaneously or at intervals and for varying periods. They have him wired to EKG and EEG monitors to facilitate giving the maximum pain without killing him.

As the final scenes unfold, Galt's fellow strikers along with Dagny hatch the plan to rescue him from his captors. The situation of the government is desperate because the chaos in the countryside is mounting and no one actually

---

[31] This very idea (forced rule) seems to have been introduced by Plato in *The Republic*. For a discussion see Roderick T. Long, "Forced to Rule: *Atlas Shrugged* as a Response to Plato's *Republic*," Younkins, Chapter 8.

knows what to do. In the irony of the moment Dr. Stadler has inadvertently set a sequence of actions that results in the destruction of the last link over the Mississippi River, the famous Taggart Bridge, by the other "invention" resulting from his research, the Xylophone. It is a device designed for use in subduing masses of people and cities and towns through wave technology allowing areas to be reduced to dust in an instant. The game is really already up for the statists, but they persist in various groupings in trying to maintain some last vestige of control, especially with reference to Galt whom they all know is their only hope for recovery. The certainty, and therefore the urgency, they have about this has been born out of and grows from the famous speech in the text of the novel. It was delivered from Galt's apartment in New York using a radio frequency unknown to the outside world and powered by his motor so as to reach the entire country.

The speech has done several things. First it has ripped the mask off the government's robbery of the people in the name of "the common good." It has also revealed the incompetency of the cadre of rulers (we now know them as "czars") and their mass of bureaucrats who facilitate the various directives. The speech also left the unmistakable impression that Galt knows what to do to rescue the situation, thus making his persona a focus of hope and morale for the masses. But, it has struck fear and loathing into the statist planners and the looters and moochers and crony-capitalists who benefit from the current arrangements. The problem is that time is running out on what can be done when the producers have vowed no longer to produce for the benefit of such a regime. They know that if Galt cannot be "persuaded" to take charge, their goose is cooked and their lives are worthless. Dr. Ferris paints the picture:

> "We want you to take full power over the economy of the country. We want you to become a dictator. We want you to rule. Understand? We want you to give orders and to figure out the right orders to give. What we want, we mean to get. Speeches, logic, arguments or passive obedience won't save you now. We want ideas—or else. We won't let you out of here until you tell us the exact measures you'll take to save our system. Then we'll have you tell it to the country over the radio." He raised his wrist, displaying a stop-watch. "I'll give you thirty seconds to decide whether you want to start talking right now. If not, then we'll start. Do you understand?" (p. 1140)

Three men watch and listen to the pitiless cycle of pain and release, then pain again and release and the beating of his heart, the gasp of his lungs. Wesley Mouch, James Taggart and Dr. Ferris play the sadistic and deadly game of pushing Galt to the edge of death and releasing him. At one point Mouch cries out, "Don't kill him! Don't dare kill him! If he dies, we die!" Taggart on the other hand is wanting to see more pressure applied. He virtually snarls, "No! It's not enough! I don't want him to obey! I want him to believe! To accept! To want to accept! We've got to have him work for us voluntarily!"

Suddenly there is a realization among them that the machine has ceased its deadly assault upon Galt's heaving body. The generator that supplied power has gone out. The technician in charge of the equipment is at a loss to explain or remedy what has happened. "The man was not a trained electrician; he had been chosen, not for his knowledge, but for his uncritical capacity for pushing any buttons; the effort he needed to learn his task was such that his consciousness could be relied upon to have no room for anything else. He opened the rear panel of the machine and stared in bewilderment at the intricate coils: he could find nothing visibly out of order." (p. 1143) As the men engage in loud and angry recriminations against one another for not having knowledge to carry on with their mission, a voice rises above the cacophony. It is Galt. Through labored breathing he deliberately instructs them on what is wrong with the machine and what to do to get it running again. The technician stands in silence for a moment looking into Galt's eyes and suddenly drops his tools and runs from the room. Galt laughs. The other three look at one another hesitantly, except for Taggart, who insists they must go on as he drops to the floor and picks up tools to fix the machine. The other two demur and begin to suggest waiting till the next day to continue, but Taggart is intent on carrying on NOW! The others realize something is happening to Taggart and warn that they must not do anything that might kill Galt. He cries out, "I don't care! I want to break him! I want to hear him scream! I want—"
"And then it was Taggart who screamed. It was a long, sudden, piercing scream, as if at some sudden sight, though his eyes were staring at space and seemed blankly sightless. The sight he was confronting was within him. The protective walls of emotion, of evasion, of pretense, of semi-thinking and pseudo-words,

built up by him through all of his years, had crashed in the span of one moment—the moment when he knew that he wanted Galt to die, knowing fully that his own death would follow." (p. 1145)

The realization in Taggart's mind at once reveals his own sordid character and that which he sees in Galt. He knows who is James Taggart and who is John Galt:

> He was suddenly seeing the motive that had directed all the actions of his life. It was not his incommunicable soul or his love for others or his social duty or any of the fraudulent sounds by which he had maintained his self-esteem: it was the lust to destroy whatever was living, for the sake of whatever was not. It was the urge to defy reality by the destruction of every living value, for the sake of proving to himself that he could exist in defiance of reality and would never have to be bound by any solid, immutable facts. A moment ago, he had been able to feel that he hated Galt above all men, that the hatred was proof of Galt's evil, which he need define no further, that he wanted Galt to be destroyed for the sake of his own survival. Now he knew that he had wanted Galt's destruction at the price of his own destruction to follow, he knew that he had never wanted to survive, he knew that it was Galt's greatness he had wanted to torture and destroy—he was seeing it as greatness by his own admission, greatness by the only standard that existed, whether anyone chose to admit it or not: the greatness of a man who was master of reality in a manner no other had equaled. In the moment when he, James Taggart, had found himself facing the ultimatum: to accept reality or die, it was death his emotions had chosen, death, rather than surrender to that realm of which Galt was so radiant a son. In the person of Galt—he knew—he had sought the destruction of all existence. (p. 1145)

Another visceral vision born of years of ignoring the value of words in favor of emotions forced him to see another face:

> He was no longer able to summon the fog to conceal the sight of all those blind alleys he had struggled never to be forced to see: now, at the end of every alley, he was seeing his hatred of existence—he was seeing the face of Cherryl Taggart with her joyous eagerness to live and that it was this particular eagerness he had always wanted to defeat—he was seeing his face as the face of a killer whom all men should rightfully loathe, who destroyed values for being values, who killed in order not to discover his own irredeemable evil. "No . . ." he moaned, staring at that vision, shaking his head to escape it. "No . . . No . . ." "Yes," said Galt. He saw Galt's eyes looking straight at his, as if Galt were seeing the things he was seeing. "I told you that on the radio, didn't I?" said Galt. (p. 1146)

As Taggart sinks to the floor in demented torment the other two men quickly retrieve him and leave the room promising to be back, but they know they will not be able to face again what they have seen there. "Their only certainty was that they had to escape from that cellar—the cellar where the living generator was left tied by the side of the dead one."

Chapter 9 - The Man Who Loved His Life

When the famous speech in *Atlas Shrugged* begins, the world is in chaos and along with it the USA. Mr. Thompson, the head of state, is scheduled to speak on the world crisis. His radio transmission is jammed and despite his loud and abusive insistence that communication be restored all are left in suspension until a voice comes through loud and clear. Only three people outside Galt's Gulch recognize it—Dagny Taggart, Eddie Willers, and Dr. Robert Stadler. John Galt has at last reached that point at which he had aimed for twelve years—the removal of the victims of collective greed. What's left is his true enemy and betrayer (Stadler), the only object left in the world that wants from it (Dagny), and the man he has been talking to throughout the story (Willers) as he worked for Taggart Transcontinental and sought to stop its motive power while "winning" its Chief of Operations. He begins appropriately, "For twelve years, you have been asking: Who is John Galt? This is John Galt speaking. I am the man who loves his life. I am the man who does not sacrifice his love or his values. I am the man who has deprived you of victims and thus has destroyed your world, and if you wish to know why you are perishing—you who dread knowledge—I am the man who will now tell you." (p. 1009) And it takes more than two hours of radio time and sixty pages in the Centennial Edition to tell them!

The speech, of course, is the distillation of Rand's Objectivism, now being explained in the abstract language of the philosophers and moralists and even preachers and prophets. The story of the novel has the purpose of unveiling the world that must follow from the accomplishment of the goals set by the "enemies of the mind," as Rand sees them. The speech is the indictment brought against those who have now arrived at the world their own philosophy demanded, aided and abetted by Galt's acceleration of the deterioration through removal of the "men of the mind." As Francisco d'Anconia stated earlier in our survey, the world is getting just what it deserved from imbibing at the well of irrationality (as Rand sees it). In stark black and white it looks like this:

> You have heard it said that this is an age of moral crisis. You have said it yourself, half in fear, half in hope that the words had no meaning. You have cried that man's sins are destroying the world and you have cursed

human nature for its unwillingness to practice the virtues you demanded. Since virtue, to you, consists of sacrifice, you have demanded more sacrifices at every successive disaster. In the name of a return to morality, you have sacrificed all those evils which you held as the cause of your plight. You have sacrificed justice to mercy. You have sacrificed independence to unity. You have sacrificed reason to faith. You have sacrificed wealth to need. You have sacrificed self-esteem to self-denial. You have sacrificed happiness to duty. (pp. 1009-1010)

Galt declares that all the world has been calling virtuous is now in the place of rule and the supposed "enemy" has been vanquished. The voice on the radio says, now see what you have!

Galt continues by explaining the nature of the strike he has caused. It is a strike by those who do not recognize the claim of "need" as binding on another's mind or the claim that a single individual can be "owned" by another human being or the claim that the "duty to serve" requires living without joy or happiness. In short, "We are on strike against self-immolation. We are on strike against the creed of unearned rewards and unrewarded duties. We are on strike against the dogma that the pursuit of one's happiness is evil. We are on strike against the doctrine that life is guilt." (p. 1010) The direction of the strike has been reversed, in the way we have seen throughout the narrative, so that the world may see in stark reality what it produces:

There is a difference between our strike and all those you've practiced for centuries: our strike consists, not of making demands, but of granting them. We are evil, according to your morality. We have chosen not to harm you any longer. We are useless, according to your economics. We have chosen not to exploit you any longer. We are dangerous and to be shackled, according to your politics. We have chosen not to endanger you, nor to wear the shackles any longer. We are only an illusion, according to your philosophy. We have chosen not to blind you any longer and have left you free to face reality—the reality you wanted, the world as you see it now, a world without mind. (pp. 1010-1011)

What follows from this, as it probably seems obvious to most that it must, is the necessity of wrestling with the moral code that delivers such a result. Throughout the novel the "good" has been constantly torn between the code of the collective and the code of the men of the mind. Just exactly what is the "good" in such a struggle? Rand's thesis in all her philosophical discussions is that "spirit" and physical reality must not be separated, so that one is torn between the "ghost" without a body (that is, intellectual, philosophical, or theological constructs that do not translate into a living reality of goodness) and the physical actions involved in work and labor divorced from the creative power of the mind. These two ends of the continuum produce the strange clash of two irrational possibilities to define the good: "The good, say the mystics of spirit, is God, a being whose only definition is that he is beyond man's power to conceive—a definition that invalidates man's consciousness and nullifies his concepts of existence. The good, say the mystics of muscle, is Society—a thing which they define as an organism that possesses no physical form, a super-being embodied in no one in particular and everyone in general except yourself." (p. 1027) Each "possibility" in this dichotomy is "mystical" for Galt and Rand because they produce what the novel's story reveals. Galt says that this struggle was introduced to mankind by those who say that morality is derived from the fact that a person's life belongs to God on the one hand and/or those who say that that same person's life belongs to one's neighbor.[32] This juxtaposition of choices results in the strange and, for Galt, intolerable situation that one is trapped "between those who preached that the good is self-sacrifice for the sake of ghosts in heaven and those who preached that the good is self-sacrifice for the sake of incompetents on earth. And no one came to say that your life belongs to you and that the good is to live it." (pp. 1011-1012) Both these sides are agreed, he says, on the idea that no morality can come from reason—"in reason there is no reason to be moral."

The Morality of Reason

Galt then proceeds to show that this cannot be true to life or morality in the world we have been given. Man cannot survive in this reality without his mind, like an animal born with instincts and tools in his physical make-up suited to that survival. Man can only survive as himself by the use of his mind. "Life is given to him, survival is not. His body is given to him, its sustenance is not. His mind is given to him, its content is not. To remain alive, he must act, and before

---

[32] If you think this is extreme, research the 2012 Democratic National Convention and their video presentation promoting the idea that government is the only thing to which we all belong.

he can act he must know the nature and purpose of his action. He cannot obtain his food without a knowledge of food and of the way to obtain it. He cannot dig a ditch—or build a cyclotron—without a knowledge of his aim and of the means to achieve it. To remain alive, he must think." (p. 1012) Reason, furthermore, is volitional, that is chosen. One does not think automatically as if it were a mechanical process or the instinct born into the nature of an animal. Man is a being of "volitional consciousness...The function of your stomach, lungs or heart is automatic; the function of your mind is not. In any hour and issue of your life, you are free to think or to evade that effort. But you are not free to escape from your nature, from the fact that reason is your means of survival—so that for you, who are a human being, the question 'to be or not to be' is the question 'to think or not to think.'" (p. 1012)

It follows that such a being does not follow a behavior pattern automatically. He/she chooses to behave according to a code of values. "'Value' is that which one acts to gain and keep, 'virtue' is the action by which one gains and keeps it. 'Value' presupposes an answer to the question: of value to whom and for what? 'Value' presupposes a standard, a purpose and the necessity of action in the face of an alternative. Where there are no alternatives, no values are possible." (p. 1012) Here Galt states clearly the fundamental "value" at the heart of *Atlas Shrugged*:

> There is only one fundamental alternative in the universe: existence or non-existence—and it pertains to a single class of entities: to living organisms. The existence of inanimate matter is unconditional, the existence of life is not; it depends on a specific course of action. Matter is indestructible, it changes its forms, but it cannot cease to exist. It is only a living organism that faces a constant alternative: the issue of life or death. Life is a process of self-sustaining and self-generated action. If an organism fails in that action, it dies; its chemical elements remain, but its life goes out of existence. It is only the concept of "Life" that makes the concept of 'Value' possible. It is only to a living entity that things can be good or evil. (pp. 1012-1013)

Contrary to what most would contend, Galt says, it is not an instinctual behavior to love life. To love life is not the automatic response of self-preservation that unerringly knows what to do to survive, for it requires knowledge. It is not desire to live, because desire cannot supply the knowledge necessary to life. It cannot be equated with fear of death, for this is not the same as desire for life or a love of it. Man has the power to both enhance and improve his life and to destroy it (unlike an animal), and destruction has been his choice throughout most of history.

Like a latter-day prophet the voice on the radio waves exhorts:

> Man has been called a rational being, but rationality is a matter of choice—and the alternative his nature offers him is: rational being or suicidal animal. Man has to be man—by choice; he has to hold his life as a value—by choice; he has to learn to sustain it—by choice; he has to discover the values it requires and practice his virtues—by choice. A code of values accepted by choice is a code of morality. Whoever you are, you who are hearing me now, I am speaking to whatever living remnant is left uncorrupted within you, to the remnant of the human, to your mind, and I say: There is a morality of reason, a morality proper to man, and Man's Life is its standard of value. All that which is proper to the life of a rational being is the good; all that which destroys it is the evil. Man's life, as required by his nature, is not the life of a mindless brute, of a looting thug or a mooching mystic, but the life of a thinking being—not life by means of force or fraud, but life by means of achievement—not survival at any price, since there's only one price that pays for man's survival: reason. (pp. 1013-1014)

The essence of this code is that man cannot attempt to live as anything other than what he is without contradicting the nature of existence itself. This is the attempt to deny that "A is A" and that "Either-Or" is a choice that must be made and that the "Law of Non-Contradiction" will not permit two formulations of the same reality to occupy the same space and time. In *Atlas Shrugged*, of course, the argument is over whose "reason" or whose judgment is to be followed. Galt answers emphatically, "Yours," for "No matter how vast your knowledge or how modest, it is your own mind that has to acquire it. It is only with your own knowledge that you can deal. It is only your own knowledge that you can claim to possess or ask others to consider. Your mind is your only judge of truth—and if others dissent from your verdict, reality is the court of final appeal. Nothing but a man's mind can perform that complex, delicate, crucial process of identification which is thinking. Nothing can direct the process but his own judgment. Nothing can direct his judgment but his moral integrity." (p. 1017) It follows that moral integrity is the property of the individual and does not exist apart from individual choice, least of all as a kind of collective wisdom or received "moral instinct." It is not "social." Consequently, "A rational process is a moral process. You may make an error at any step of it, with nothing to protect you but your own severity, or you may try to cheat, to fake the evidence and evade the effort of the quest—but if devotion to truth is the hallmark of morality, then there is no greater, nobler, more heroic form of devotion than the act of a man who assumes the responsibility of thinking." (p. 1017) Galt says this is man's basic virtue, accepting the responsibility of thinking. On the other hand the fundamental nature of evil ("the source of all evils") is "that nameless act which all of you practice, but struggle never to admit: the act of blanking out, the willful suspension of one's consciousness, the refusal to think—not blindness, but the refusal to see; not ignorance, but the refusal to know. It is the act of unfocusing your mind and inducing an inner fog to escape the responsibility of judgment—on the unstated premise that a thing will not exist if only you refuse to identify it, that A will not be A so long as you do not pronounce the verdict 'It is.'" (pp. 1017-1018) This right and obligation of the individual to formulate or accept as valid a moral code the negation of life, for "When a man declares: 'Who am I to know?'—he is declaring: 'Who am I to live?'" (p. 1018)

Galt then juxtaposes this obligation of the individual to reason through to moral conclusions the notions of commandment and faith. It would at first appear that Rand is using his voice to throw out religious claims, and this is probably her own intent. However, it is clear that the language she/he is using treats commandment as a forced response, not a proposition to be weighed and accepted or rejected, a rational process. If a "commandment" requires a "forced response," then it cannot be "moral." If is to be obeyed without understanding, it is not "moral." The same goes for the "mysticism" she attaches to "faith." This is the sense of obligation to accept as fact something as true to reality simply because someone said it was so. Such "mysticism" naturally bypasses the mind in favor of outside authority, producing and unthinking "morality." From this array of premises flows the summary statement about the nature of life and living:

> To live, man must hold three things as the supreme and ruling values of his life: Reason—Purpose—Self-esteem. Reason, as his only tool of knowledge—Purpose, as his choice of the happiness which that tool must proceed to achieve—Self-esteem, as his inviolate certainty that his mind

is competent to think and his person is worthy of happiness, which means: is worthy of living. These three values imply and require all of man's virtues, and all his virtues pertain to the relation of existence and consciousness: rationality, independence, integrity, honesty, justice, productiveness, pride. (p. 1018)

It follows from this that such a person will not live frivolously, indolently, or in dissipation, because it is inconsistent with the very nature of life itself. Such is the morality that comes from reason. The person who holds unswervingly to such a creed does not kowtow to received opinion or majoritarian morality simply because it is hard to swim against the tide, for he knows that reality will vindicate his rightness and goodness. As Galt sees it virtue of this type is productive of life—a key distinction, for virtue is not an end in itself but the means to life. He insists that even in his present situation, as an outcast from society and one hunted by the government, he has achieved the goal of his living:

Are you beginning to see who is John Galt? I am the man who has earned the thing you did not fight for, the thing you have renounced, betrayed, corrupted, yet were unable fully to destroy and are now hiding as your guilty secret, spending your life in apologies to every professional cannibal, lest it be discovered that somewhere within you, you still long to say what I am now saying to the hearing of the whole of mankind: I am proud of my own value and of the fact that I wish to live. (p. 1021)

Happiness

That goal, strangely enough, is what he and Rand call "happiness"—a theme which we have previously addressed. It is here that true happiness as it is intended in the rational life is discussed at length. It is not to be achieved (and it is achieved, not received) by the pursuit of whims of emotion and the faking of reality, the pursuit of "whatever irrational wishes you might blindly attempt to indulge." It cannot be had in the fortune you did not earn or the love you do not deserve (because you have hidden your corruption like James Taggart). "Happiness is a state of non-contradictory joy—a joy without penalty or guilt, a joy that does not clash with any of your values and does not work for your own destruction, not the joy of escaping from your mind, but of using your mind's fullest power, not the joy of faking reality, but of achieving values that are real, not the joy of a drunkard, but of a producer." (p. 1022)

100

Such a person does not expect someone else to live for his or her happiness any more than he will do so. "Just as I support my life, neither by robbery nor alms, but by my own effort, so I do not seek to derive my happiness from the injury or the favor of others, but earn it by my own achievement. Just as I do not consider the pleasure of others as the goal of my life, so I do not consider my pleasure as the goal of the lives of others." (p. 1022) Galt is bold to call the symbol of such relationships *the Trader.*" In keeping with Rand's refusal to divide the material from the spiritual, Galt refers to this as being a trader of the spirit, and then explains: "A trader is a man who earns what he gets and does not give or take the undeserved. A trader does not ask to be paid for his failures, nor does he ask to be loved for his flaws. A trader does not squander his body as fodder or his soul as alms. Just as he does not give his work except in trade for material values, so he does not give the values of his spirit—his love, his friendship, his esteem—except in payment and in trade for human virtues, in payment for his own selfish pleasure, which he receives from men he can respect." (p. 1022) In this light, "selfish" takes on a very nuanced meaning, for this "pleasure" is something produced by "virtue"—the search for and the production of the highest values of the mind and body. When Galt finds men and women of this same mindset he enters into relationships of mutual benefit and pleasure. When he does not, he simply goes about his own purposeful existence. He does not force anyone into his way of thinking or acting.

> I let dissenters go their way and I do not swerve from mine. I win by means of nothing but logic and I surrender to nothing but logic. I do not surrender my reason or deal with men who surrender theirs. I have nothing to gain from fools or cowards; I have no benefits to seek from human vices: from stupidity, dishonesty or fear. The only value men can offer me is the work of their mind. When I disagree with a rational man, I let reality be our final arbiter; if I am right, he will learn; if I am wrong, I will; one of us will win, but both will profit. (pp. 1022-1023)

The coercion of the use of the mind for the profit of others, especially the "common good," pervades the narrative of *Atlas Shrugged* and is the driving incentive of the men of the mind to have a go at changing the world. But it is a peculiarly non-violent approach that Galt has taken. His ultimatum is "our work or your guns." He will not tolerate both. "You can choose either; you can't have both." He goes on to explain that the ones with the guns have ruled through the fear of death. If the men of the mind return, they will offer life to those who receive them back gladly. Once again the theme of "life" predominates:

> You have never discovered that achieving life is not the equivalent of avoiding death. Joy is not "the absence of pain," intelligence is not "the absence of stupidity," light is not "the absence of darkness," an entity is not "the absence of a nonentity." Building is not done by abstaining from demolition; centuries of sitting and waiting in such abstinence will not raise one single girder for you to abstain from demolishing—and now you can no longer say to me, the builder: "Produce, and feed us in exchange for our not destroying your production." I am answering in the name of all your victims: Perish with and in your own void. Existence is not a negation of negatives. (p. 1024)

The Morality of Death

What follows is an exploration of the "Morality of Death" to which the purveyors of fear and coercion are committed. Once again it is pertinent to note that Rand's perceptions of what this morality entails are based on premises that go undefended here. The "Morality of Death" is so denominated because, "Damnation is the start of your morality, destruction is its purpose, means and end. Your code begins by damning man as evil, then demands that he practice a good which it defines as impossible for him to practice. It demands, as his first proof of virtue, that he accept his own depravity without proof. It demands that he start, not with a standard of value, but with a standard of evil, which is himself, by means of which he is then to define the good: the good is that which he is not." (p. 1025) Here is Galt's declaration at length:

> The name of this monstrous absurdity is Original Sin. A sin without volition is a slap at morality and an insolent contradiction in terms: that which is outside the possibility of choice is outside the province of morality. If man is evil by birth, he has no will, no power to change it; if he has no will, he can be neither good nor evil; a robot is amoral. To hold, as man's sin, a fact not open to his choice is a mockery of morality. To hold man's nature as his sin is a mockery of nature. To punish him for a crime he committed before he was born is a mockery of justice. To hold him guilty in a matter where no innocence exists is a mockery of reason. To destroy morality, nature, justice and reason by means of a single concept is a feat of evil hardly to be matched. Yet that is the root of your code.
>
> Do not hide behind the cowardly evasion that man is born with free will, but with a "tendency" to evil. A free will saddled with a tendency is like a game with loaded dice. It forces man to struggle through the effort of

102

playing, to bear responsibility and pay for the game, but the decision is weighted in favor of a tendency that he had no power to escape. If the tendency is of his choice, he cannot possess it at birth; if it is not of his choice, his will is not free. (p. 1025)

It is paramount at this point to make no mistake about what Galt/Rand is saying here. We quote this passage extensively to be fair and to prepare for our later analysis of this take on human existence. Here we find the premises that lead to the analysis of the source of the evils being denounced throughout *Atlas Shrugged* and Rand's other writings:

What is the nature of the guilt that your teachers call his Original Sin? What are the evils man acquired when he fell from a state they consider perfection? Their myth declares that he ate the fruit of the tree of knowledge—he acquired a mind and became a rational being. It was the knowledge of good and evil—he became a moral being. He was sentenced to earn his bread by his labor—he became a productive being. He was sentenced to experience desire—he acquired the capacity of sexual enjoyment. The evils for which they damn him are reason, morality, creativeness, joy—all the cardinal values of his existence. It is not his vices that their myth of man's fall is designed to explain and condemn, it is not his errors that they hold as his guilt, but the essence of his nature as man.

Whatever he was—that robot in the Garden of Eden, who existed without mind, without values, without labor, without love—he was not man. Man's fall, according to your teachers, was that he gained the virtues required to live. These virtues, by their standard, are his Sin. His evil, they charge, is that he's man. His guilt, they charge, is that he lives.

They call it a morality of mercy and a doctrine of love for man. No, they say, they do not preach that man is evil, the evil is only that alien object: his body. No, they say, they do not wish to kill him, they only wish to make him lose his body. They seek to help him, they say, against his pain—and they point at the torture rack to which they've tied him, the rack with two wheels that pull him in opposite directions, the rack of the doctrine that splits his soul and body. They have cut man in two, setting one half against the other.

They have taught him that his body and his consciousness are two enemies engaged in deadly conflict, two antagonists of opposite natures, contradictory claims, incompatible needs, that to benefit one is to injure the other, that his soul belongs to a supernatural realm, but his body is an evil prison holding it in bondage to this earth—and that the good is to defeat his body, to undermine it by years of patient struggle, digging his way to that glorious jail-break which leads into the freedom of the grave.

They have taught man that he is a hopeless misfit made of two elements, both symbols of death. A body without a soul is a corpse, a soul without a body is a ghost—yet such is their image of man's nature: the battleground of a struggle between a corpse and a ghost, a corpse endowed with some evil volition of its own and a ghost endowed with the knowledge that everything known to man is non-existent, that only the unknowable exists. (p. 1025- 1026)

The terrible dichotomy Galt describes here has its dread consequences in the struggle for meaning in man's existence. He sees two sides at war over the spoils produced by man's mind, when it is free from this torture chamber. These two parties (for lack of a better word) or "teachers" as he calls them both hold man in thrall to the Morality of Death: "the mystics of spirit and the mystics of muscle, whom you call the spiritualists and the materialists, those who believe in consciousness without existence and those who believe in existence without consciousness. Both demand the surrender of your mind, one to their revelations, the other to their reflexes." (p. 1027) Man in this condition cannot be said to actually "live" in any meaningful sense for "he is the passively ravaged victim of a battle between a robot and a dictaphone." (p. 1027) Such a state leads to a monstrous distortion of the "good" by the push-pull of outside forces. Consequently man's mind must be subordinated unthinkingly to either "God's will" or "Society," as quoted in the lines above. The standards of value(s) are either to be accepted "on faith" or "must be obeyed as a primary absolute." Both leave man as "an abject zombie who serves a purpose he does not know, for reasons he is not to question." (p. 1027) Man's "reward" is either an ethereal existence "beyond the grave" or a blessing to passed along "to his great-grandchildren."

Sacrifice and Selfishness

At this point the voice of Galt (Can this possibly escape a comparison to the voice speaking from Horeb?) intones a long discussion of the clash between the meaning of the terms "selfishness" and "sacrifice." It is clear from the thousand or so pages the reader has absorbed up to this point that terminology is everything in ferreting out meaning and intent in the context of the novel. Words do not always carry their common referents in *Atlas Shrugged*. For those who are not well-versed in this issue, the necessity of such re-tooling of the language comes from the deliberate intention of the political left to distort language usage so as to import effects into the conversation that would otherwise be thought

104

unacceptable.[33]   In the world created by "newspeak," as it is called in *1984*, "sacrifice" takes on a completely new garb:

> "Sacrifice" does not mean the rejection of the worthless, but of the precious. "Sacrifice" does not mean the rejection of the evil for the sake of the good, but of the good for the sake of the evil. "Sacrifice" is the surrender of that which you value in favor of that which you don't. If you exchange a penny for a dollar, it is not a sacrifice; if you exchange a dollar for a penny, it is. If you achieve a career you wanted, after years of struggle, it is not a sacrifice; if you then renounce it for the sake of a rival, it is. If you own a bottle of milk and give it to your starving child, it is not a sacrifice; if you give it to your neighbor's child and let your own die, it is. If you give money to help a friend, it is not a sacrifice; if you give it to a worthless stranger, it is. If you give your friend a sum you can afford, it is not a sacrifice; if you give him money at the cost of your own discomfort, it is only a partial virtue, according to this sort of moral standard; if you give him money at the cost of disaster to yourself—that is the virtue of sacrifice in full. If you renounce all personal desire and dedicate your life to those you love, you do not achieve full virtue: you still retain a value of your own, which is your love. If you devote your life to random strangers, it is an act of greater virtue. If you devote your life to serving men you hate—that is the greatest of the virtues you can practice. (p. 1028)

In the world of *Atlas Shrugged* this standard leads to a renouncing of "self" that includes the renunciation of the individual right to make moral judgments apart from the collective because he/she has no right to such independence. "Give to that which you do not enjoy, serve that which you do not admire, submit to that which you consider evil—surrender the world to the values of others, deny, reject, renounce your *self.* Your self is your mind; renounce it and you become a chunk of meat ready for any cannibal to swallow." (p. 1030) Galt then makes it clear he understands this renunciation to be a sacrifice of one's mind to that of others with this consequence: "Those who start out by saying, 'It is selfish to pursue your own wishes, you must sacrifice them to the wishes of others'—end up by saying: 'It is selfish to uphold your convictions, you must sacrifice them to the convictions of others.'…You are asked to sacrifice your intellectual integrity, your logic, your reason, your standard of truth—in favor of

---

[33] Orwell's *1984* is a classic treatment of this issue. See also Jonah Goldberg, *Liberal Fascism: The Secret History of the American Left from Mussolini to the Politics of Meaning* and Gene Edward Veith, *Modern Fascism: The Threat to the Judeo-Christian*

becoming a prostitute whose standard is the greatest good for the greatest number." (p. 1030)

Such an immoral use of the language, from Galt's perspective, must be submitted to intensive questioning:

> "I, who do not accept the unearned, neither in values nor in *guilt*, am here to ask the questions you evaded. Why is it moral to serve the happiness of others, but not your own? If enjoyment is a value, why is it moral when experienced by others, but immoral when experienced by you? If the sensation of eating a cake is a value, why is it an immoral indulgence in your stomach, but a moral goal for you to achieve in the stomach of others? Why is it immoral for you to desire, but moral for others to do so? Why is it immoral to produce a value and keep it, but moral to give it away? And if it is not moral for you to keep a value, why is it moral for others to accept it? If you are selfless and virtuous when you give it, are they not selfish and vicious when they take it? Does virtue consist of serving vice? Is the moral purpose of those who are good, self-immolation for the sake of those who are evil? (p. 1031)

The answer to these questions is supplied throughout the novel and specified here. It involves an upside down rationalization of the system that takes from the producers and gives to the looters and moochers who are considered somehow more worthy than the producers:

> No, the takers are not evil, provided they did not earn the value you gave them. It is not immoral for them to accept it, provided they are unable to produce it, unable to deserve it, unable to give you any value in return. It is not immoral for them to enjoy it, provided they do not obtain it by right. Such is the secret core of your creed, the other half of your double standard: it is immoral to live by your own effort, but moral to live by the effort of others—it is immoral to consume your own product, but moral to consume the products of others—it is immoral to earn, but moral to mooch—it is the parasites who are the moral justification for the existence of the producers, but the existence of the parasites is an end in itself—it is evil to profit by achievement, but good to profit by sacrifice—it is evil to create your own happiness, but good to enjoy it at the price of the blood of others. (p. 1031)

This sense of the moral is behind the creedal statement, "From each according to his ability to each according to his need." In practice such a morality becomes a monstrosity:

Worldview. The writings of Saul Alinsky show the leftist intent and practice and the 2012 presidential campaign is rife with its use.

Under a morality of sacrifice, the first value you sacrifice is morality; the next is self-esteem. When need is the standard, every man is both victim and parasite. As a victim, he must labor to fill the needs of others, leaving himself in the position of a parasite whose needs must be filled by others. He cannot approach his fellow men except in one of two disgraceful roles: he is both a beggar and a sucker. You fear the man who has a dollar less than you, that dollar is rightfully his, he makes you feel like a moral defrauder. You hate the man who has a dollar more than you, that dollar is rightfully yours, he makes you feel that you are morally defrauded. The man below is a source of your guilt, the man above is a source of your frustration. You do not know what to surrender or demand, when to give and when to grab, what pleasure in life is rightfully yours and what debt is still unpaid to others—you struggle to evade, as 'theory,' the knowledge that by the moral standard you've accepted you are guilty every moment of your life, there is no mouthful of food you swallow that is not needed by someone somewhere on earth—and you give up the problem in blind resentment, you conclude that moral perfection is not to be achieved or desired, that you will muddle through by snatching as snatch can and by avoiding the eyes of the young, of those who look at you as if self-esteem were possible and they expected you to have it. Guilt is all that you retain within your soul—and so does every other man, as he goes past, avoiding your eyes. Do you wonder why your morality has not achieved brotherhood on earth or the good will of man to man? (p. 1033)

Love and Objectivity

This last is the indictment of the would-be utopian planners of economies in the mold of those which are collapsing around the world in *Atlas Shrugged*. It was the death of the Twentieth Century Motor Company and the fate of all societies which have tried it in the past. They depended on the love of men and women for their fellows without discrimination or cause or reason. And if it was not forthcoming voluntarily the planners and societal governors have always been prepared to use coercion and the fear of it to produce the supposed beneficial results, as if the one can exist without the other. Galt says that cannot be possible in the world of human existence, for "Love is the expression of one's values, the greatest reward you can earn for the moral qualities you have achieved in your character and person, the emotional price paid by one man for the joy he receives from the virtues of another." (p. 1034) Just as fear is produced by cause (otherwise it is considered paranoia), love is produced by cause as well, unless the language and the value has been corrupted. Once again Galt rescues language from this abyss:

> Your morality tells you that the purpose of love is to set you free of the bonds of morality, that love is superior to moral judgment; that true love transcends, forgives and survives every manner of evil in its object, and the greater the love the greater the depravity it permits to the loved. To love a man for his virtues is paltry and human, it tells you; to love him for his flaws is divine. To love those who are worthy of it is self-interest; to love the unworthy is sacrifice. You owe your love to those who don't deserve it, and the less they deserve it, the more love you owe them—the more loathsome the object, the nobler your love—the more unfastidious your love, the greater the virtue—and if you can bring your soul to the state of a dump heap that welcomes anything on equal terms, if you can cease to value moral values, you have achieved the state of moral perfection. (p. 1034)

Those who have been reduced to this state of mind cannot be expected to make choices in love or sexuality that exalt human nature or life, they can only debase it. Love cannot be emptied of objective value and filled with subjectivism any more than building a skyscraper can. It is wishing instead of creating. Galt switches us quickly between the realms of subjectivist feelings and "faith" to the world of productivity and objective values. Once again we are in Rand's Aristotelian world of non-contradiction where A is A and the choice is Either-Or. For once one accepts some wish as reality in one area one soon finds the compromise has contaminated all things it touches. "Whenever you committed the evil of refusing to think and to see, of exempting from the absolute of reality some one small wish of yours, whenever you chose to say: Let me withdraw from the judgment of reason the cookies I stole, or the existence of God, let me have my one irrational whim and I will be a man of reason about all else—that was the act of subverting your consciousness, the act of corrupting your mind." (p. 1037) A simple and ancient axiom applies: "You cannot have your cake and eat it too." The opposite also applies: "You cannot eat your cake before you have it."

Love without cause in Rand's thought is no more possible than the existence of rail line and airplanes and industrial plants without cause. This perception of reality is a rejection of objectivity and in the speech of John Galt looks a lot like what is today called post-modernism. Galt asserts that creating

108

such a "reality" is in fact a mission of the men of muscle, those who would control the masses by taking from them the ability to think for themselves.

> "If you doubt that such is their purpose, observe with what passionate consistency the mystics of muscle are striving to make you forget that a concept such as 'mind' has ever existed. Observe the twists of undefined verbiage, the words with rubber meanings, the terms left floating in midstream, by means of which they try to get around the recognition of the concept of 'thinking.' Your consciousness, they tell you, consists of 'reflexes,' 'reactions,' 'experiences,' 'urges,' and 'drives'—and refuse to identify the means by which they acquired that knowledge, to identify the act they are performing when they tell it or the act you are performing when you listen. Words have the power to 'condition' you, they say and refuse to identify the reason why words have the power to change your— blank-out. A student reading a book understands it through a process of— blank-out. A scientist working on an invention is engaged in the activity of—blank-out. A psychologist helping a neurotic to solve a problem and untangle a conflict, does it by means of—blank-out. An industrialist— blank-out—there is no such person. A factory is a 'natural resource,' like a tree, a rock or a mud puddle.[34] The problem of production, they tell you, has been solved and deserves no study or concern; the only problem left for your 'reflexes' to solve is now the problem of distribution. Who solved the problem of production? Humanity, they answer. What was the solution? The goods are here. How did they get here? Somehow. What caused it? Nothing has causes. (p. 1043)

And finally, to sew it up in a neat package: "And to forestall any inquiry into the cause of the difference between a jungle village and New York City, they resort to the ultimate obscenity of explaining man's industrial progress—skyscrapers, cable bridges, power motors, railroad trains—by declaring that man is an animal who possesses an 'instinct of tool-making.'" (p. 1044)

What could possibly possess those who concoct such a plot? "Make no mistake about the character of mystics. To undercut your consciousness has always been their only purpose throughout the ages—and power, the power to rule you by force, has always been their only lust." (p. 1044) Furthermore, "Every dictator is a mystic, and every mystic is a potential dictator. A mystic craves obedience from men, not their agreement. He wants them to surrender their consciousness to his assertions, his edicts, his wishes, his whims—as his

---

[34] Ron Sider actually takes this position (that "factories" are among the fundamental rights to be classified as "needs") in some of his latest writings. See our *Seeking the City* from Kregel, Spring, 2013.

consciousness is surrendered to theirs. He wants to deal with men by means of faith and force—he finds no satisfaction in their consent if he must earn it by means of facts and reason." (p. 1045) Such men and women find fulfillment in the coercion of others, in the enslavement of their labors, in the directing of the minutiae of their lives. They cannot be bought off by money nor assuaged by any accretion of power for their lust for it is endless. Stating the horror of it Galt asserts: "You who are craven enough to believe that you can make terms with a mystic by giving in to his extortions—there is no way to buy him off, the bribe he wants is your life, as slowly or as fast as you are willing to give it up—and the monster he seeks to bribe is the hidden blank-out in his mind, which drives him to kill in order not to learn that the death he desires is his own. (p. 1046) The ages of history reveal the truth:

"Destruction is the only end that the mystics' creed has ever achieved, as it is the only end that you see them achieving today, and if the ravages wrought by their acts have not made them question their doctrines, if they profess to be moved by love, yet are not deterred by piles of human corpses, it is because the truth about their souls is worse than the obscene excuse you have allowed them, the excuse that the end justifies the means and that the horrors they practice are means to nobler ends. The truth is that those horrors are their ends. (p. 1046)

The Sanction of the Victim

It is but a short step from the realization to which we have now come to the conclusion that such men of muscle require one thing from their victims: compliance, or in the language of Rand and Galt, "the sanction of the victims." That consists in the willingness to go on producing and inventing and creating in vague guiltiness for having achieved some good that now belongs to everyone more than it does to the producer. Galt taught the strikers what the game was all about: "When you clamor for public ownership of the means of production, you are clamoring for public ownership of the mind. I have taught my strikers that the answer you deserve is only: 'Try and get it.'" (p. 1049) Twelve years before he had walked out on such a scheme. Now the others have. Galt invites the world to consider what it would find outside if they had never existed:

110

If you want to know what you lost when I quit and when my strikers deserted your world—stand on an empty stretch of soil in a wilderness unexplored by men and ask yourself what manner of survival you would achieve and how long you would last if you refused to think, with no one around to teach you the motions, or, if you chose to think, how much your mind would be able to discover—ask yourself how many independent conclusions you have reached in the course of your life and how much of your time was spent on performing the actions you learned from others—ask yourself whether you would be able to discover how to till the soil and grow your food, whether you would be able to invent a wheel, a lever, an induction coil, a generator, an electronic tube—then decide whether men of ability are exploiters who live by the fruit of your labor and rob you of the wealth that you produce, and whether you dare to believe that you possess the power to enslave them. Let your women take a look at a jungle female with her shriveled face and pendulous breasts, as she sits grinding meal in a bowl, hour after hour, century by century—then let them ask themselves whether their "instinct of tool-making" will provide them with their electric refrigerators, their washing machines and vacuum cleaners, and, if not, whether they care to destroy those who provided it all, but not "by instinct." (pp. 1048-1049)

In the narrative of the novel we have seen that the incompetents of the business, political, and cultural world propose to rule and organize and direct the ones whose competence is finally seen to be indispensable. They have the guns and propose to coerce the minds of those who do not comply and they rely on guilt and envy and resentment and a host of hateful characteristics in man to accomplish their purposes.

You propose to establish a social order based on the following tenets: that you're incompetent to run your own life, but competent to run the lives of others—that you're unfit to exist in freedom, but fit to become an omnipotent ruler—that you're unable to earn your living by the use of your own intelligence, but able to judge politicians and to vote them into jobs of total power over arts you have never seen, over sciences you have never studied, over achievements of which you have no knowledge, over the gigantic industries where you, by your own definition of your capacity, would be unable successfully to fill the job of assistant greaser. (p. 1049)

Galt calls this the "cult of zero-worship," a religion of man in the image of non-existence, of "impotence." Its hymn of degradation points to the "congenital dependent." It is in conclusion:

Your image of man and your standard of value, in whose likeness you strive to refashion your soul. "It's only human," you cry in defense of any depravity, reaching the stage of self-abasement where you seek to make

111

the concept 'human' mean the weakling, the fool, the rotter, the liar, the failure, the coward, the fraud, and to exile from the human race the hero, the thinker, the producer, the inventor, the strong, the purposeful, the pure—as if "to feel" were human, but to think were not, as if to fail were human, but to succeed were not, as if corruption were human, but virtue were not—as if the premise of death were proper to man, but the premise of life were not. (pp. 1049-1050)

Those who hold such a view of man will accept the mystics of muscle as rulers and will support them in rule as long as they get what they consider their "fair share" of whatever can be extracted from the producers. They are like the beggars who accost people on the streets aggressively seeking hand-outs and shaming those who will not comply with their wishes. They concur with the politicians who decry the "greed" of the "rich" and imply that the poor are their victims. These all cry and plead for "help" in the tone of a threat and count on the guilt created by the false morality of "sacrifice" and the obliteration of self respect and independent moral judgment to achieve the objective of a hand out. Addressing these moochers and looters, Galt declares, "You expect us to feel guilty of our virtues in the presence of your vices, wounds and failures—guilty of succeeding at existence, guilty of enjoying the life that you damn, yet beg us to help you to live." (p. 1050) Once again the question reverberates and is answered:

Did you want to know who is John Galt? I am the first man of ability who refused to regard it as guilt. I am the first man who would not do penance for my virtues or let them be used as the tools of my destruction. I am the first man who would not suffer martyrdom at the hands of those who wished me to perish for the privilege of keeping them alive. I am the first man who told them that I did not need them, and until they learned to deal with me as traders, giving value for value, they would have to exist without me, as I would exist without them; then I would let them learn whose is the need and whose the ability—and if human survival is the standard, whose terms would set the way to survive. (p. 1050)

Conclusion

The final stage of the radio address from Galt's Gulch is an exhortation to make a choice that is clear and concrete. It is a call to all those who have wavered between two opinions and those who have secretly understood in some sense Galt's message throughout their lives, perhaps without the ability to articulate it and/or the courage to force the issue in their private and public experience. He calls for a "judgment" of the mind followed by an action of the body that will

112

celebrate the superiority of life over death. No compromise is permitted when these are at stake. "The man who refuses to judge, who neither agrees nor disagrees, who declares that there are no absolutes and believes that he escapes responsibility, is the man responsible for all the blood that is now spilled in the world." (p. 1054) This is because there is a right and a wrong in every dispute and the man who is wrong at least has respect for the issue and makes a choice. The compromiser is the one who believes there really is no truth to be found and is the truly evil one. The principle involved is universally applicable: "When men reduce their virtues to the approximate, then evil acquires the force of an absolute, when loyalty to an unyielding purpose is dropped by the virtuous, it's picked up by scoundrels—and you get the indecent spectacle of a cringing, bargaining, traitorous good and a self-righteously uncompromising evil." (pp. 1054-1055

In his final appeal Galt points to his own example and urges those who are fearful and uncertain to follow his example and find a new existence for themselves as he did. He assures them it is not too late, not least because he and the men and women on strike will return when the collapse of the present system forces the rulers to abandon their guns. He does not claim they need perfection in what he has discovered to make the first steps. All they need to do is *take* the first steps.

Evil is not in ignorance but in the refusal to know in deference to "feeling":

> Give the benefit of the doubt to those who seek to know; but treat as potential killers those specimens of insolent depravity who make demands upon you, announcing that they have and seek no reasons, proclaiming, as a license, that they 'just feel it'—or those who reject an irrefutable argument by saying: 'It's only logic,' which means: 'It's only reality.' The only realm opposed to reality is the realm and premise of death. (p. 1059)

Recognize the system you have:

> "You did not care to compete in terms of intelligence—you are now competing in terms of brutality. You did not care to allow rewards to be won by successful production—you are now running a race in which rewards are won by successful plunder. You called it selfish and cruel that men should trade value for value—you have now established an unselfish society where they trade extortion for extortion. Your system is a legal civil war, where men gang up on one another and struggle for possession of the law, which they use as a club over rivals, till another gang wrests it from their clutch and clubs them with it in their turn, all of

them clamoring protestations of service to an unnamed public's unspecified good. You had said that you saw no difference between economic and political power, between the power of money and the power of guns—no difference between reward and punishment, no difference between purchase and plunder, no difference between pleasure and fear, no difference between life and death. You are learning the difference now. (pp. 1065-1066)

Stop supporting your destroyers:

If, in the chaos of the motives that have made you listen to the radio tonight, there was an honest, rational desire to learn what is wrong with the world, you are the man whom I wished to address. By the rules and terms of my code, one owes a rational statement to those whom it does concern and who're making an effort to know. Those who're making an effort to fail to understand me, are not a concern of mine.

I am speaking to those who desire to live and to recapture the honor of their soul. Now that you know the truth about your world, stop supporting your own destroyers. The evil of the world is made possible by nothing but the sanction you give it. Withdraw your sanction. Withdraw your support. Do not try to live on your enemies' terms or to win at a game where they're setting the rules. Do not seek the favor of those who enslaved you, do not beg for alms from those who have robbed you, be it subsidies, loans or jobs, do not join their team to recoup what they've taken by helping them rob your neighbors. One cannot hope to maintain one's life by accepting bribes to condone one's destruction. Do not struggle for profit, success or security at the price of a lien on your right to exist. Such a lien is not to be paid off; the more you pay them, the more they will demand; the greater the values you seek or achieve, the more vulnerably helpless you become. Theirs is a system of white blackmail devised to bleed you, not by means of your sins, but by means of your love for existence. (pp. 1066-1067)

Make a choice, not a compromise:

That choice is yours to make. That choice—the dedication to one's highest potential—is made by accepting the fact that the noblest act you have ever performed is the act of your mind in the process of grasping that two and two make four. Whoever you are—you who are alone with my words in this moment, with nothing but your honesty to help you understand—the choice is still open to be a human being, but the price is to start from scratch, to stand naked in the face of reality and, reversing a costly historical error, to declare: "I am, therefore I'll think." (p. 1058)

Chapter 10 - The anti-Anti-Christ

As the voice of John Galt ceased to vibrate the airwaves, reaction in the halls of power was immediate and predictable from those who had long-since become the muscle-men Galt portrays them to be. It was not unlike the reaction to *Atlas Shrugged* when it came to publication in 1957. Was that for real? Did we really hear that? And in answer, We seem to have heard it. We couldn't help it. One lesser technician tried to bolt the room and was ordered to stay put by Mr. Thompson, who then proceeded to demand an explanation for the occurrence. James Taggart spoke for most: "Why is he so sure he's right? Who is he to go against the whole world, against everything ever said for centuries and centuries? Who is he to know? Nobody can be sure! Nobody can know what's right! There isn't any right!" (p. 1071) Then the spin-control (an anomalous phrase here we know) began. How do we play this out? Immediately refute the speech, someone yells. Shut down the radio music that has resumed, says another. Thompson has the answer: Don't let the public think they hadn't authorized the speech or were unable to stop it. "Broadcasts as usual!" ordered Mr. Thompson. "Tell them to go on with whatever programs they'd scheduled for this hour! No special announcements, no explanations! Tell them to go on as if nothing had happened!" (p. 1071) Eugene Lawson protests loudly that they cannot appear to endorse the speech. "It's horrible! It's immoral! It's selfish, heartless, ruthless! It's the most vicious speech ever made! It . . . it will make people demand to be happy!" (p. 1071) Thompson soothes the group by pointing out he had no intention of endorsing any of it, because it was just a speech. And round the room leaders of each faction offer reasons why their followers will not endorse it either. Dr. Ferris sums it up with, "People are too dumb to understand it."

Much of this kind of invective greeted the book when it first arrived on bookshelves around the US. Not one "critic" gave it a favorable review, from the "right" or the "left." It was a profound disappointment to Rand and her inner circle of friends. But the book quickly sold its first run and went on to be a *New York Times* bestseller and has now become the most circulated hardcover book in the history of publishing except for the Bible. Rand's disappointment, by all accounts available to us, did not stem primarily from personal rejection but from the realization that her hope for respect among the intellectual establishments of the day, respect that could get her views a fair hearing at least, was not in the offing. The upshot of this rejection, in her opinion, was that the American economic and spiritual haven to which she had fled from the Soviet slave state was bound on a course that would inevitably lead to the degradation and sorrow and bloodshed she had left behind. It was beyond all reason as she saw it that not one literary or political or cultural pundit would take a stand with her. Instead she was personally and professionally excoriated in the most harsh and vitriolic terms. The words of Dagny Taggart in the midst of the conversation above (first paragraph) echo what happened when *Atlas Shrugged* appeared: "You know the truth, all of you," she said, "and so do I, and so does every man who's heard John Galt! What else are you waiting for? For proof? He's given it to you. For facts? They're all around you. How many corpses do you intend to pile up before you renounce it— your guns, your power, your controls and the whole of your miserable altruistic creed? Give it up, if you want to live. Give it up, if there's anything left in your mind that's still able to want human beings to remain alive on this earth!" (p. 1073)

To Rand, and many others, the actual facts of the past century in the world would seem to be irrefutable. The cult of collectivism pitted against the freedom and creativity of the individual in economics and politics has produced nothing but misery where it has actually been placed in operation. It has no track record to commend it. It leaves death and poverty and planetary pollution in its wake. It pits people and constituencies against one another in resentment and envy. It grows government to totalitarian dimensions because there is no way to stop regulating and taxing, since it is regulation and regimentation and taxation that cause the misery in the first place and reduces all to the same pitiful level, except for the aristocracies of power.[35] The insidious nature of the monster is that it convinces masses of people philosophically and religiously (this term is intended to convey the meaning of Rand's "mysticism") that this way is the best way

---

[35] For the full treatment of these issues, see our *Seeking the City*, from Kregel, Spring, 2013.

because it satisfies some sense of the need to "look out for the little guy" while being best for the most in a modern society. In addition it satisfies the need to assuage a vague guilt in the Western world about the prosperity that has seemed to overtake this civilization in the pat 300 years. In short, it answers to the Galt-ian concern for what's really "wrong with the world." Surely the "answer" cannot be that one needs to be more "selfish." Surely it cannot be that the individual should be exalted over the society, or more hopefully, the "community." And, especially for the serious Christian, surely it cannot be in the exaltation of the mind of man over "faith." Some even go so far as to label John Galt as the equivalent of Anti-Christ, the creation of an atheistic mind gone to seed on capitalism and materialistic greed. Surely the "answer" to the world's problems economically and politically cannot be found in a man deemed to be so perfect as to be incomparable in his dedication to virtue, his fearless rejection of the "evil" he sees, the clarity with which he sees the "truth," and the fierceness of his love of life on this earth! Most disturbing of all, how is it possible to find truth in a character who rejects "original sin" as a fundamental category for evaluating man on this earth?

The remainder of our book will explore these issues, and any others that bear upon these basics, and seek to offer a ground for learning from the good of *Atlas Shrugged* while clearly critiquing the areas that are incompatible with Christianity and with philosophical consistency. This chapter will explore the almost eerie comparison of the narrative journey in the book compared to the Bible and the character of John Galt in it as a "Christ" figure, a device used repeatedly in the Western world of literature and art and politics. We have found no evidence that Rand intentionally built in all that we will touch on here, but the similarities and differences are so striking that we have found ourselves unable to ignore them. Rand, of course, at various points in the speeches of the book refers straightforwardly to apparent biblical and Christian themes with pejorative intent. Our next chapter will analyze some of the impressions she is working from in her dislike for what she sees in the Christian tradition. At the very least the use made over two thousand years in the West of the figurative "Christ" in art and literature is plain even in a cursory reading of *Atlas*. That fact has led in our thinking to some other striking reflections as we have structured this study. Stay with us for the ride!

Rand's stated purpose for writing her greatest novel was to put her objectivism on display in such a way as to concretize that which would come across as heavy and dense abstractions in a philosophical treatise. She has chosen a narrative structure to convey the truth of what to her is a coherent system of thought. She couches it in standard literary forms using mystery, romance, intrigue, human failing, heroism, and action sequences to carry a storyline and a reasoned argument to a plausible conclusion. It should be obvious to anyone familiar with the nature of Western literature from the earliest stages of human thought that the narrative style has always carried the mostest-for-the-mostest when it comes to communicating on a level that reaches more than an intellectual constituency that handles heavy abstractions well. She succeeded beyond any reasonable expectation in doing just that by taking us by the hand and getting us to read 1200 pages of narrative and philosophy that is the *sine qua non* of the genre—except for the Bible. And this is the uncanny truth: the Bible is just such a book as well. It is a grand narrative written over a period of more than a thousand years with one great theme and one great philosophical and theological purpose that goes from the Garden to the Great City. The marvel of the Bible is that it has the hand of many humans upon it and purports to be the result of the work of the one living God upon the minds and mouths of those writers and speakers, yet the narrative is consistent in its theme and builds to its climax and finish with the same kind of intensity seen in *Atlas*. We would commend a reading of it by *Atlas* readers from cover to cover repeatedly just as they may have treated Rand's work.[36] The dramatic meta-narrative of Scripture is overwhelming in its consistency and literary power, but it will not yield its fruit to the merely curious or the nibbler any more than objectivism does to a like reader of *Atlas Shrugged*.

The story line is about a mysterious personage who appears in the text from time to time as either a referent in conversation or preaching or promise or

---

[36] To assure yourself that you are reading the various parts in their context, get a good annotated study Bible like the *English Standard Bible* or the *Holman Christian Standard Bible*.

118

poetry or prophecy. That person is associated with the hopes and aspirations of the whole world which is languishing in its desperate situation and looking for answers to what is wrong with it. Various heroes of conviction and virtue along with known flaws arise and fall as generations pass. No change, just repeats and reruns. One man is the hope of his father for the relief of toil and sorrow in work, but all he ends up saving are seven others after passing through a horrendous chaotic flood. A city for refuge and renown is set up in a fertile plain with a tower that invites the gods to come down and rest, but it ends up being the place of mass confusion and disappointment. An ideal, almost utopian society, is established with a view to righting the wrongs that have gone before. More heroic and ignoble characters pass through the narrative of the rise and fall of that nation. As the world of an apparent ideal civilization collapses, and its institutions fail to provide sustenance and prosperity as planned, there are increasing longings and hopes that somehow someone can rescue the situation. The utopian dream has fallen on the inability of the characters in the story to remain faithful to their highest ideals and aspirations.

Finally, two-thirds of the way through the story that *person* arrives, as he does in the novel, and proves to be the consummate man with the answer for the world's need. But he is not here to force himself upon the world. He speaks as no one has ever spoken. He is "able" in the face of the impossible. He has the perfect answer for every inquiry and attempt to divert his attention. He has the courage of conviction unto death. He is unafraid of the consequences of his singular vision of what is wrong and what must happen. He goes about gathering one and another here and there who will go with him and learn from him. He makes of them a fellowship built around his teaching of the truth, while he himself needs no one to teach him. And then he falls into the hands of evil men who kill him out of envy and lust for power and position. He disappears from view while others carry on his mission, instructed to imitate him in the world and not let themselves be compromised in any way by the world of power and politics and lying philosophies and religions. The parallels to Galt are striking. In the final denouement he returns to establish a city based on what he taught and died for.

John Galt also promises such a scenario for those who follow his lead and answer the invitation he has given to make a choice and refuse to be victimized further:

> Go on strike—in the manner I did. Use your mind and skill in private, extend your knowledge, develop your ability, but do not share your achievements with others. Do not try to produce a fortune, with a looter riding on your back. Stay on the lowest rung of their ladder, earn no more than your barest survival, do not make an extra penny to support the looters' state. Since you're captive, act as a captive, do not help them pretend that you're free. Be the silent, incorruptible enemy they dread. When they force you, obey—but do not volunteer. Never volunteer a step in their direction, or a wish, or a plea, or a purpose. Do not help a holdup man to claim that he acts as your friend and benefactor. Do not help your jailers to pretend that their jail is your natural state of existence. Do not help them to fake reality...If you find a chance to vanish into some wilderness out of their reach, do so, but not to exist as a bandit or to create a gang competing with their racket; build a productive life of your own with those who accept your moral code and are willing to struggle for a human existence. You have no chance to win on the Morality of Death or by the code of faith and force; raise a standard to which the honest will repair: the standard of Life and Reason. Act as a rational being and aim at becoming a rallying point for all those who are starved for a voice of integrity—act on your rational values, whether alone in the midst of your enemies, or with a few of your chosen friends, or as the founder of a modest community on the frontier of mankind's rebirth. (p. 1067)

And finally, when all else has collapsed he promises that he and the others will return, when the muscle-men lay down their arms:

> When the looters' state collapses, deprived of the best of its slaves, when it falls to a level of impotent chaos, like the mystic-ridden nations of the Orient, and dissolves into starving robber gangs fighting to rob one another—when the advocates of the morality of sacrifice perish with their final ideal—then and on that day we will return. We will open the gates of our city to those who deserve to enter, a city of smokestacks, pipe lines, orchards, markets and inviolate homes. We will act as the rallying center for such hidden outposts as you'll build. With the sign of the dollar as our symbol—the sign of free trade and free minds—we will move to reclaim this country once more from the impotent savages who never discovered its nature, its meaning, its splendor. (p. 1067)

Surely this must be the vision of Anti-Christ. As attractive as that dismissive conclusion might be to some, it simply cannot be made to match the dismal and fearful picture of the "man of sin" in Scripture. That figure is clearly a coercive and totalitarian ruler with worldwide ambitions and delusive power

120

whose goal is enslavement of the world through a "mark" that limits what any can do in trade or economics or political power. The monstrous "city," which stands in as a whorish caricature of the New Jerusalem, is a debauched and dissipated city of stolen wealth and slave labor with degraded values of every kind. None of these powers or such dissipation or degradation of values interest John Galt. In fact, he stands for the exact opposite. He wishes to be left alone by such powers and has set himself to have such an existence, even if he must secede from the present structure altogether. He is passive-resistive. He is non-violent by conviction. He is willing to defend himself from direct attack and others from attack if they are innocent. He will not be the first to use force. He is ready to risk his own life to make the world freer for all and unable to support evil. He seeks no empire nor anything that he himself has not produced. All of this characterizes Galt, and it looks a lot more like Christ than it does the "man of sin." Furthermore, his advice to those waiting for his return sounds a lot like Jesus praying for his disciples that they will be in but not of the world. It is clear that Rand has created a unique character and a unique picture of the world to which he aspires, as does she. The real question to be asked is how is this attainable without biblical presuppositions. We will address that issue later.

Pertinent also to this characterization of Galt is the entire scenario of the mysterious broadcast to all the USA that supersedes all communication for a period of over two hours. It speaks from the air above a nation and addresses the fundamental issues of existence and insists that no other way forward is possible. It admits no compromise and gives no quarter. It bids to define the very nature of life and contends that all else is a way of death on this earth. It frightens and angers and disconcerts and puzzles and instructs and exhilarates the audience depending on their presuppositions in hearing it. No face is seen and no likeness is projected and the impression of immense power is created while words pile upon words on and on. Though it would seem Rand cannot have meant it so, this begs in our thinking to be compared to Sinai and the experience of Israel before the mountain that smoked and flamed and had a voice that thundered on and on in such a manner as to cause the congregation to plead with Moses not to insist they go on listening. Galt would clearly deny that he was imitating YHWH on the mountain, but the impression is uncanny and it contributes to our understanding of what it is that Rand saw about "faith" and "mysticism" that was repulsive. We will have more to say on this theme later also.

Finally, it is surely of concern that Galt and Rand deny and excoriate their version and interpretation of "original sin." We will be addressing this issue more as we go along. For now we note that reading carefully through the speech in the section that directly addresses the issue, one is forced to decide whether the problem for Rand is failure to understand what is at stake in the Garden and the subsequent development of it in the Bible, or whether she is truly unaware that sin is endemic to the human condition. Galt admits that the history of mankind confirms that he is the only animal that must make choices and use his mind to survive, to live. No other animal does—they act out of instinct, they are behavioral in nature, and they always fight for actual survival. Man is a reasoning creature, and has consistently chosen over time and history to be destructive of his own existence. Galt never labels this tendency as "sin." One wonders what Rand would call it under direct questioning, other than irrationality. But what is it that makes this a persistent characteristic of man in all societies? It is possible she would simply attribute it to the teaching of "mystics" throughout man's long development from being influenced by shamans and witch doctors to the medieval scholastics and modern religious fanatics. It is clear that there is some flaw that is causing this repetitive activity and Rand does not deny it. But her heroic characters, and especially Galt, who was her lifelong quest in real life, is actually a paragon of virtue in the classic sense of that word. He has somehow achieved this clear knowledge of truth and the unsullied ability to be loyal to it and all those who choose the same course. And yet he contemplates actual death toward the end of the speech, a death that could happen in the midst of the quest for the goal:

> All life is a purposeful struggle, and your only choice is the choice of a goal. Do you wish to continue the battle of your present or do you wish to fight for my world? Do you wish to continue a struggle that consists of clinging to precarious ledges in a sliding descent to the abyss, a struggle where the hardships you endure are irreversible and the victories you win bring you closer to destruction? Or do you wish to undertake a struggle that consists of rising from ledge to ledge in a steady ascent to the top, a struggle where the hardships are investments in your future, and the victories bring you irreversibly closer to the world of your moral ideal, and

should you die without reaching full sunlight, you will die on a level touched by its rays? Such is the choice before you. Let your mind and your love of existence decide. (p. 1068)

This is not the voice of the Anti-Christ. It is more that of the anti-Anti-Christ of our title. It is hard not to say what Jesus said to an inquirer one day: "You are not far from the kingdom of God."

Chapter 11 - The Egoist

Neither Ayn Rand nor her ideal man would shun the moniker in our title above. In fact, Rand used the term to distinguish between her understanding of "selfishness" and the concept of egotism. John Galt is the supreme egoist, though his role had been invented in *The Fountainhead*. Howard Roark in that story was the man who was purely concerned about his own values and person and simply did not take notice of the opinions or activities of others as they might pertain to his own value judgments and creative endeavors. When asked by his greatest critic, Ellsworth Toohey, what he (Roark) thought of him (expecting to get an earful), the egoist responded that he did not think of him at all. The self-important Toohey saw this as more than an indignity to his person. It was a moral failing. The same is constantly said about John Galt, whose character is an advancement on Roark designed to engage the ideal man in struggle to change the context in which he lives. Roark endures. Galt sets out to set right what's "wrong with the world." The character of both men is supreme confidence that they are capable in themselves of discerning the good and choosing it, of ignoring the carping of critics in favor of personal critical judgments about reality, and using this knowledge and critical ability to provide for themselves without resort to the pity and charity of others. The motto is clear and succinct: "I swear—by my life and my love of it—that I will never live for the sake of another man, nor ask another man to live for mine."

Rand never cut corners in her portrayal of this vow in action, and in her public acknowledgement of its raw, in-your-face style. It seems likely to us that she intended its stark fault-line as a shout above the noisy public din of her most despised concept, altruism. Altruists hold that individuals have a moral obligation to help, serve, or benefit others, if necessary, at the sacrifice of self interest. Auguste Comte's version of altruism calls for living for the sake of others. One who holds to either of these ethics is known as an "altruist." The word "altruism" (*French, altruisme, from autrui: "other people", derived from Latin alter: "other"*) was coined by Auguste Comte, the French founder of positivism, in order to describe the ethical doctrine he supported. He believed that individuals had a moral obligation to renounce self-interest and live for others. Comte says, in his *Catéchisme Positiviste*, that:

> [The] social point of view cannot tolerate the notion of rights, for such notion rests on individualism. We are born under a load of obligations of every kind, to our predecessors, to our successors, to our contemporaries. After our birth these obligations increase or accumulate, for it is some time before we can return any service.... This ["to live for others"], the definitive formula of human morality, gives a direct sanction exclusively to our instincts of benevolence, the common source of happiness and duty. [Man must serve] Humanity, whose we are entirely.[37]

The *Catholic Encyclopedia* says that for Comte's altruism, "The first principle of morality...is the regulative supremacy of social sympathy over the self-regarding instincts." Author Gabriel Moran (professor in the department of Humanities and the Social Sciences, New York University) says, "The law and duty of life in altruism [for Comte] was summed up in the phrase: Live for others."[38] In general scholars, philosophers, and commentators on the subject follow substantially the same understanding that Rand has: altruism is literally living for others rather than oneself and discounting whether one finds personal joy or satisfaction in the actions taken. One's personal happiness cannot be allowed to intrude upon the obligation to live for others exclusively.

Most critics of Rand and her hero John Galt find the ideal of "selfishness," when compared to the altruism defined above, to be repugnant. We might say in light of our previous chapter, Galt may not be the Anti-Christ, but he is an egotistical and selfish, even hateful man unworthy of serious consideration, especially by anyone seeking a Christian worldview. Two general reflections, however, speak to this concern. First, Rand is specifically reactive in her philosophy and novels to the idea of societal and governmental coercion to collectivist public policy, though we also see in *Atlas* the attempt to implement the altruistic ideal in a single company setting. She is aware of the nature of family and friendship and their mutual obligations, but she does not see them in the same

---

[37] August Comte, *Catéchisme positiviste* (1852) or *Catechism of Positivism*, trans. R. Congreve, (London: Kegan Paul, 1891).

[38] Quoted on Wikipedia site. This is a general statement that many would agree is accurate and Rand is reacting to this characterization.

light as the attempt to implement societal altruism as public policy. More on this below. Second, Rand is reacting to a version of Christian ethics that is decidedly un-biblical and requires serious refutation. The generally pervasive ideal of "other-driven" service to the church and/or mankind in general is typically irrational and "mystical" (Rand's terminology) in formulation and impossible to implement in any rational way among the general populous. This is what spawned the language of egoism and selfishness in Rand's philosophy. Most certainly she did not mean by either term what the term "egotist" designates by dictionary definition: chiefly, "self-absorbed" or "self-seeker" or even "narcissistic." On the contrary, the antagonists of her novels display this personality disorder. Her heroes mostly want to be left alone to be productive and creative, celebrating the joy of their work, and reaping its rewards to be used as they think best. Their willingness to take responsibility for their own opinions and decision-making and their desire to make decisions about the dispersal of the profits of their labor is labeled by others as "selfish," and Rand simply says, yes it is.

Of course, the "self" in Rand is virtually synonymous with rational consciousness. To be selfish is to place primary dependency for interaction on the world in the hands of one's own mind and not that of another or the collective of whatever makeup. This comes before all other considerations in decision making because one must think to make choices. Simply "going along" because conventional "wisdom" dictates certain courses of action is a robotic "life" not worthy of the name. It is also irresponsible for it diverts consequences from oneself to the ubiquitous and amorphous "they." They say, they did, they decided, or worse, put "everyone" in the place of "they." It follows that one can then claim in the face of disaster, it wasn't my fault! I'm not to blame! Somebody help me! Of course, this thinking does not apply to situations that are truly out of the control of anyone capable of preventing them. But the real-life application of the principle in *Atlas* is the famous tunnel disaster that one group wants to call unavoidable and that Rand shows to be the logical progression of a chain of events linked to non-thinking robotic actions based on refusal to be "selfish" in the Randian sense. Of course, though Rand does not go out of her way in the novel to assert this selfishness against the general notion of "god," the underlying

126

philosophy posits no god-inference from rational data and ignores any implications that might flow from that possibility. Within the framework of her worldview the idea of selfish concern for personal freedom of the individual and accountability to oneself for choices without interference from others--so long as no harm is done to others through force or fraud--apart from any collective notion of good and evil is not an offensive concept.

With reference to the second consideration above, Rand's selfishness is not incompatible with biblical ideas of man in the image of God held accountable on an individual basis for his good and evil choices and/or his failure to gain knowledge of the right and/or wise action. Scripture is clear that regardless of the collective to which one belongs, personal accountability is fundamental to man's existence on this earth and for eternity beyond. He is expected to practice the law of God to "live" (Lev. 18:5), choose "life" and not death (Dt. 30:19), refuse to follow "the many" to do evil or go to court with them to pervert good into evil (Ex. 23:2),[39] and exercise individual courage in the face of even overwhelming opposition (Num. 14:36, 37). This last incident is the classic parallel to Rand's heroic characters in their struggle against those who constantly carp about how selfish it is for them to think they could be right when everyone is opposed to them. On the other hand the Old Testament teaches one must love the neighbor and also the "stranger" among the people (Lev. 19:18, 34).

Many, of course, in Christian circles contend that the ethic of Jesus in this area is superior to the Old Testament. They cite his own example as the one who gave his life "for others" and taught his disciples to do likewise. Specifically, among other similar passages, it can be noted that God "gave" His Son (Jn. 3:16), He walked among men as a "servant" (Jn. 13:14-17) and bid his followers do the same, He died for those he loved (Gal. 2:20), He told them to "deny" themselves daily (Lk. 9:23) and "take up the Cross" lest one "lose himself" (v. 25, ESV), and His own Apostles taught the churches to "love one another" and give attention to the things of others as they do to themselves (Phil. 2:4). We would not contend

---

[39] This is clearly the mandate against the right of the societal or political collective to demand loyalty in an evil matter.

there is anything amiss in asserting that both testaments of the Christian Scriptures encourage concern and action on behalf of others besides oneself.

On the other hand, the last book of the Bible exhorts the churches in chapters 2 and 3 to repent of behaviors and beliefs that are un-Christian and promises eternal rewards to individuals who join Jesus Christ in "overcoming."[40] The presumption here must be that even in the church community individual accountability trumps the collective responsibility. The New Testament, perhaps even more than the Old Testament, emphasizes the necessity of individual choice and action regardless of collective issues. Jesus says with reference to family and friends that He must have the primary position of loyalty (Mt. 10:31-39), even to the point of separation and death as an individual from this nearest form of collective life. One cannot give Caesar what belongs to God (Mt. 22:21). Repentance and faith for salvation are always individual and personal and cannot be done one for another (Acts 2:38). Most important of all is the clear evidence that Jesus himself was not an altruist. He did not "live for others." He lived and died to fulfill a destiny set from eternity (Heb. 12:2) that included his own "joy" at the prospect of what He was doing. This is the "joy" he sought for His own followers (Jn. 15:11; 16:24; 17:23). Fundamental to His life and death was that it was all done to please His Father (Jn. 8:28, 29; 10:15-18). He sought to "please" one "other" Who gave Him the agenda for action and decision and timing and gave Him the ones who were hearing and receiving His teaching. In our context here, this is the equivalent of a value system that guides a rational process, regardless of whether we posit God as the referent or that which reason can ferret out and understand. Obviously we would say that Rand and Galt need to check their premises, but that does not force them into altruism.

Altruism by its very nature would have changed Jesus' agenda while He was on this earth. The crowds seemed like "sheep without a shepherd" (Mt. 9:36) who at one point complained of the ministry of John and then of the ministry of Jesus (Mt. 11:16-19). Jesus felt compassion for them and healed and fed them, but His own enlightened understanding of them and the mission He had from the

---

[40] The admonition to each church that begins "he that overcomes" is always a singular grammatically.

Father made Him "selfish" in the Randian way—He must do the will of the Father. The crowds ate bread and were filled and sought to force Him into a kingship, and the next day came looking for the soup kitchen, and when He refused to play that role for them, they left Him flat (Jn. 6:15, 26, 27, 66). The Gospels record His repeated challenges to the crowds to take up the cross and follow, to which they responded negatively. His relationship with the national leadership was like that portrayed in *Atlas Shrugged*. Finally, they hailed Him on Sunday and called for His crucifixion on Friday. He went about His business (Jn. 10:18) as an other-directed Son of the Father. This is not altruism. It is what Paul saw and described as the process of justification (Rom. 3:21-26), a *transaction* that remains mysterious even as we applaud it. It is much closer to Galt's understanding of "trading" than it is to any altruistic "living for others." Jesus did not die willy-nilly for an example to follow of selfless and unconditional loving of "others." He died in purposeful fulfillment of an eternal plan that would without fail bring "many" to salvation and glory and restore ultimately the created order. Whatever else we call this, it must be called a rational construct that makes sense within the context of the narrative of Scripture. It makes the universe far more "benevolent" than Rand imagined in her world, but it does not encourage faith in altruistic collectivism of any kind. That does not work in either reality.

There nevertheless remains an ongoing residual of "compassionate" feeling that is the legacy of Christian concern for other people that condemns outright the "egoism" and "selfishness" of John Galt. Rand consistently in her public presentations and written creations made her language on the subject sharp and transparent. She never backs down and permits no "compromise." Of course, her life bore the scars of Soviet harshness and she was an unabashed believer in the hope that was America. When she saw that the hope was itself sick and on a course that she felt would lead to the death of an idea that could save mankind from untold misery, she engaged in unparalleled polemic to get a hearing. We use "unparalleled" advisedly, for nothing like this has appeared before or since. Yet it continues to excite interest and draw shocked invective. The arguments above appear to us as very straightforward and leave us only with the softer criticisms.

Social and familial relationships appear to some to be lacking or severely truncated in Rand's view of "life" as she calls it. How do "selfish" people love one another and form families and communities? How can "traders" relate to "traders" as living beings with emotions and desires? For Rand these relationships should always reflect the same rational considerations that economic and workplace trade-offs do. Love may seem to be an irrational longing and need for the other and clearly outside the box of rational explanation. But Rand would say that the failure to control these "feelings" within the bounds of reason is a part of the "wrong with the world" situation. Men and women enter into sexual unions without thought and evaluation based on their highest aspirations. This leads to marriages like the Reardens and James Taggart and liaisons like Taggart and Lillian Rearden. On the other hand, Dagny Taggart (the stand-in for Rand herself) is torn between three loves that begin in childhood with Francisco d'Anconia, proceed to Hank Rearden in the middle of *Atlas*, and finally arrive at permanence (we presume) in John Galt. This process is somewhat reflective of Rand's own disappointments in love and marriage.

It is not a "happy" picture, and Rand herself admitted that in cases such as this one should prepare to be "judged," apparently implying that consequences would follow and one must face up to them. In other words sex and marriage are a work in progress even as "climbing the ledge" Galt mentions at the end of his speech. It is a matter of aspiration in this area even more than it is in others. What each of these men in Dagny's life exhibits, however, is the ability to know the difference between need and pity and love. One cannot have a permanent relationship based on the first two, which lead to fake relationships and real dysfunctionality. Love, on the other hand, is two people bringing together their highest aspirations in agreement and consummating that relationship sexually in a way that does not divorce one side of the relationship from the other—that is, the physical from the spiritual. This is a higher ethic than serial sexual relationships or serial marriage, but it is clearly not the biblical idea of covenant. Rand would not sanction mere physical coupling and not all "spiritual" (her use means "rational") fellowship between the sexes demand sexual union (!), but Dagny is seeking something she does not find till she meets Galt. This is an inadequate societal building block and a clearly sub-Christian ideal.

Ragnar Danneskjold and Kay Ludlow are another case altogether. They appear to have found this perfect union of mind and body and have joined for life. The woman who runs the bakery shop and is rearing two children in Galt's Gulch appears to have the same relationship with her husband. Bill Brent in the episode at the tunnel is another who has built a strong marriage and family while living the life of individual struggle. Galt himself has a high view of what the relationship with a woman should be when he simply remarks to Dagny that some in the valley have wives and children and their relationship is of a kind (in trade-offs) that he could not possibly claim from her. The book, of course, cannot cover all ground, and it is lacking in further grist for this particular mill. But it might be helpful to relate a personal story here. I (Tom) read *Atlas* in 1965 and was captivated by so much about it that as a young college student and pastor and avid reader of the Bible I was greatly influenced by its thinking. I was particularly swayed in the area of possible choices to be made for a life partner, should the opportunity ever come up. In younger experience I had experienced the waves of desire in the body and the torrents of passionate emotion in what Americans call "falling in love." Having barely "escaped" from these temporary but serious infatuations, I made a vow to God that I would never allow myself to become so enamored with the other sex again unless there was a clear compatibility with the goals and aspirations of my life in the other person. When I met my wife-to-be about a year after that, I had read *Atlas* and was reading it again. Along with two other books (both on the life of Jim Elliot) I gave it to Karen and told her to read them and we would talk, and I let her know how important they were in my thinking. In the ensuing days I tried to make it plain that our relationship, if it was to proceed, would have to be based on agreement about what our life would be about and how it might develop. No faking. No compromising. No marry the other party and hope for change. Either we are in agreement from the beginning or there is no reason to proceed. My goal was to make a lifelong commitment that, no matter what happened, would not require me to apologize for where our life went because I fooled her into marrying me or vice versa. Forty-six years later we are still married. And it has been every bit of the road we agreed to and probably worse!

I regard this as the Christian version of what Rand aspires to. It is a repudiation of the "falling in love" syndrome sold like candy-corn across America and the world and that has been syncretized into the fabric of the churches, baptized as some form of Christian love. It is the reason, as we see it that divorce is as rampant among "Evangelicals" as it is in the general population. The outcry against the "trader" mentality espoused by Galt/Rand, even in the area of sexuality, is badly overdone. As pastors we (Chad and Tom) have had our bellies full of counseling people who married with ulterior motives, who feed one another's "needs" in mutual enablement, who use sexuality as a weapon and a tool, who "fall in love" and out of love serially and move on again and again, and a host of other aberrations that are far worse than making clear what is being brought to marriage by each partner to see if there is any real compatibility and hope for covenant-keeping. People can do worse than listen to John Galt on this subject.

Finally, a word on simple friendship and community. It is clear that the "selfishness" in *Atlas* does not hinder either of these. On the contrary, it enhances and solidifies them. True friendship does not exist in a vacuum any more that a good marriage does. Community cannot be forced upon a group by fiat. If one's highest values are not mirrored in others, there is little hope for companionable and accountable friendship and there is no hope for "community" among apparently disparate individuals. *Atlas Shrugged* advocates for community (see above in the previous chapter) and friendship based on the common denominator of aspiration to attainment of valued goals and the admiration and respect built around the struggle at every level. It is not necessary to have a Galt-like super-hero leading the charge, only those who find in him an inspiration to seek their own highest level of achievement in life. Among those who are committed to that kind of "selfishness" there is already community and friendship that is only enhanced by the additions of age, gender, craft, workplace, church affiliation, and other accoutrements that make the journey and struggle easier. This is precisely the kind of "community" envisioned in the church of the New Testament. People are pulled together by aspiration to follow Christ. He has called them and they follow Him in togetherness. It is not their social condition, age, ethnicity, outside friendship or craft, or any other thing that makes them a community. It is agreement that all follow Christ to the death as their highest goal in life. They do not live for others, they live for Christ. He is the "head" of everything. Paul even calls this kind of binding in sacrifice to Christ a "rational" service of worship (Rom. 12:1, 2). Jesus himself formed this very community when he was apprised of the arrival of his (then) unbelieving family to take him away from his "selfish" ministry. His reply will seal the deal:

> [31] And his mother and his brothers came, and standing outside they sent to him and called him. [32] And a crowd was sitting around him, and they said to him, "Your mother and your brothers are outside, seeking you." [33] And he answered them, "Who are my mother and my brothers?" [34] And looking about at those who sat around him, he said, "Here are my mother and my brothers! [35] For whoever does the will of God, he is my brother and sister and mother." (Mk. 3:31-34)

Perhaps the most poignant demonstration of this kind of family kinship can be seen in the stark difference between the relationship Hank Rearden has with Tony, the Wet Nurse, and his own brother Philip. Tony earned the respect and love of a man who would not let his own brother near his mills because he was a parasite and malingerer. The two are like the sons in Jesus' parable of the two sons commanded to do their duty for their father. The one said no and repented, and the other said yes and disobeyed (Mt. 21:28-32). Jesus called this an issue of eternal significance. Christians in America and around the world could also do much worse than listening to John Galt talk about the importance of obeying one's individual perception of who their true family and friends are. Galt's criteria agrees with Jesus about the necessity of making one's highest value — in this case following Christ in doing the will of the Father--the priority when determining relationships, not some perceived collective idea of obligation and neediness.

Chapter 12 - God & Mammon

Galt's invitation to await the time when the men of the mind will return, when the looters have put down their guns, contains the promise that men and women of reason will be allowed to trade value for value without interference under the societal sign of the dollar. This sign has appeared in Galt's Gulch and imprinted on the paper of cigarettes and scrawled on the statue of Nat Taggart as a signal from Dagny. It highlights a theme that is once again expressive of Rand's fierce commitment to capitalism and in-your-face style of contrasting collectivism and its aristocracy of pull with the society of traders. She has made it clear that money is a medium for exchanging values and is degraded when it is thought of as the "root of all evil," as the antagonists of the plot call it. She is not content simply to point out that her opponents use money hypocritically even as they denounce its importance, for they use it to buy influence (pull) and "friendship" and even marriage alliances, and are as dependent upon it for survival as the alleged "selfish" industrialists and businessmen. Rand seeks consciously to knock down a supposed religious evaluation of money, which she believed was part of a systematic enslavement of the mind of man to mystical categories as opposed to reason.

Christians are rightly wary of this characterization of one of the warnings in Scripture. It is seen in the warnings to all those who prosper materially on earth or who would aspire to wealth out of their apparent poverty. Generally it takes the theme that wealth diverts man's attention from God and becomes a god. Perhaps the two most famous sayings are the one from Jesus: "You cannot serve God and mammon" (Mt. 6:24), and the one from Paul: "The love of money is a root of all kinds of evils" (1 Tim. 6:10 ESV). Francisco, we have seen, takes this last warning in the simple common vernacular, first, "Money is the root of all evil," and then the additional, supposedly corrective, "The love of money is the root of all evil," and debunks them in his speech. He does so by showing that in the first case there is a failure to understand what the actual nature of money is, and in the second case he flatly states that love of money is a virtue to the person understanding his first proposition and the nature of love. When one understands love, one sees that money is that which frees mankind from the tyranny of collectivism by giving each and every person a means of trading that which has value to oneself for that which has value to another. This is a principle to actually love and preserve, for it allows the accumulation and spread of "wealth" without fraud and coercion, and facilitates the ability of each person to concentrate on that which has true value as "wealth" to oneself.

In practical living it means that those like Paul, who worked as a leather crafter, could go about the Mediterranean world taking care of himself and his companions by selling his work and his goods for the money that provided the means of survival. Money eliminated the barter process and left him free to preach the Gospel without being beholden to patrons and the chance offerings of those who heard him on the streets or in the squares or other public forums, such as Mars Hill in Athens. In this sense one should "love" money for its ability to convert values of one party, those who sought Paul's wares and leather services, to the values of the other party, being enabled to preach the Gospel. The system of money allows one to be free without the interference of a patron, the Roman world's master of pull, or even the time consuming barter market. Rand and d'Anconia elevate this to the level of philosophical principle that is compatible with a Christian understanding of money. Jesus worked as a *tekton*[41] for his earthly father, and likely on his own after Joseph's death. He very likely supported his own family until led out in his public ministry by the Holy Spirit. Jesus and Paul have no problem at the point of understanding how money facilitates trading and exchange in honest dealing and the admiration of it in operation that can be called "love" when considering how it has benefited mankind in the widespread creation of wealth available to the largest percentage of world population in history.[42]

Many Christians, of course, look askance at the accumulation of wealth that makes one "rich" in some sense of that term, whether relatively or enormously

---

[41] This Greek term can mean "carpenter" in the common rendering, but it is not restricted simply to wood-working.

[42] We refer the reader once again to our *Seeking the City* from Kregel for the full discussion and documentation on this chapter's subject.

so. Some will suggest absolute limits on such accretions to single individuals or corporations. Others will simply support the policies of governments for efforts at redistribution of accumulated wealth in whatever form by taxation and regulation. Within the church many make efforts to use various means to make wealthy people feel guilt for their "luck" or "good fortune" in life. Others formulate theologies of varying degrees of required or expected divestiture of "surplus" goods for the benefit of the "poor." In these ways businessmen and women are made to feel like second class Christians for having as their primary goal of business "making money." By this they mean that they cannot run a business that stays in business without making a profit. The antagonists in *Atlas Shrugged* constantly inveigh against the "profit motive" as a kind of immoral, or at least amoral, value to be placed in subservience to the "common good." Some Christian theologians and spokesmen through the centuries have taken this position, idealizing the value of poverty and simplicity of living, and elevating the value and good of "meaningful" work and the "fulfillment" it brings. In all of these cases Christians find themselves quite often at a loss for words to defend both the individual and corporate accumulation of profits that constitute real wealth and the American "way of life" that so enables this process. Rand is in part reacting to this tendency of Christians to leave the field of economic comment to the collectivists and altruists and/or join them in political actions and invective against the "rich." They should not.

First, returning to the example of Jesus and Paul, any examination of the ministries of these men reveals clearly that they both benefited from the wealth accumulation of people in the first century. Jesus was supported especially by wealthy women, who would not ordinarily in the first century world have been personally and independently wealthy. They would have been inheritors of estates and/or married to wealthy men, both Jewish and possibly Hellenist. Paul experienced the same thing in his missionary travels and benefited greatly from people wealthy enough to have large houses for meeting and servants and family to make up "households." The newest work on the history of the Christian church shows clearly that the earliest converts were not merely peasants and beggars and

136

slaves and illiterate workers.[43] There is no indication that there was ever any general movement to seek divestiture of the wealth of early church members. However, they were a boon to the spread of Christianity by their generosity and hospitality. What Paul did avoid in his travels, and what Jesus criticizes at times, is the system of patronage which many Jews had tapped into and Roman citizens accepted as customary for those in the lower echelons of society—a receiving of benefaction for the "favor" of supporting the rich patron politically and culturally. Otherwise, the warnings of Scripture are for rich and poor alike to beware the seductions of money as a means of security in a world where, anciently, God said, "Man shall not live by bread alone, but by every word that comes from the mouth of God" (Dt. 8:3; Mt. 4:4; Jn. 4:34 ESV).

The two quotations above from the d'Anconia speech are enlightening in both the common misquotations. James Taggart's misquote and Rand's acceptance of it and the supposed "correction" are instructive when taken against the actual Pauline quote. Neither common version gets it right. Neither money itself nor its love is the root of "all evil." The translation we cite is the correct one and it makes no such universal claim for the denunciation of money. It says fundamentally what is illustrated in the novel and supported by the speech. The love of money is "a" root of "all kinds of evils" is a statement that requires unpacking and enfleshment even as the scene in the novel does. The manner in which some characters "love" money is diametrically opposed to what Francisco delineates. They demonstrate it when their own conversations are ended in the panic to get out of the room, leaving the only three people who do understand the proper "love" of money standing in silence. They know that the money being lost in the crash of d'Anconia stock was already worthless and cannot now be recovered, but of the entire crowd they are also the only ones proven capable of replacing it. Therefore, Francisco's motive in destroying such "wealth" is justified by his values and his own ability to reproduce it when his values for its distribution are met in a world with no guns drawn on him. The struggle for

---

[43] See Rodney Stark, *Cities of God: The Real Story of How Christianity Became an Urban Movement and Conquered Rome* (New York: HaperOne, 2007) and *The Triumph of Christianity: How the Jesus Movement Became the World's Largest Religion* (New York: HarperOne, 2011).

Rearden and Dagny is to see that their wealth is in the service of the looters and needs to be abandoned or destroyed until it can be reproduced in a different evaluation system. There is no threat to Christian thinking here.

The statement of Jesus above is also enlightening. Most Christians in our era, along with non-Christians as well, do not understand the strong implications of Jesus' teaching. The word for "serve" in the Greek is the word "bondslave." It does not mean merely a house servant or a valet or a butler or some other lowly version of common labor. It means someone whose entire existence belongs to his or her Master and Owner. One cannot be *owned* by more than one Master. It is an impossible scenario. Yet many, maybe most, modern Christians have no sense of being owned by God so that every hour of every day and every work or action is controlled and accountable to Him. They are not really "Christian" to begin with. They have a nominal relationship to the church and other "Christians," but in no sense do they consider themselves *owned* by God through Jesus Christ as Lord. From this standpoint Jesus is stating the obvious—one can only have one *owner*. Either God or something or someone else. "Mammon" here in the context is the sense of security that comes from earthly "treasures" rather than heavenly ones, those that come from being *owned* by the heavenly Master. A Christian must choose between finding security in earthly things or heavenly things. And if one is like the famous "rich young ruler," Jesus will see whether you or I are *owned* by our money and require of us what it takes to detach us from it so we might belong to Him alone.

This is a sense of valuation of the hierarchy of "goods" in our reality that fits the Randian model. Galt himself would not allow his greatest achievement to be put to a use he did not approve no matter what the cost in "money" was to him. Hank Rearden felt the same about his famous Metal and eventually followed his rational conclusions. Francisco took action on the same principle in the destruction of his family fortune. Others of the "men of the mind" did the same as they one by one dropped out of the world they saw around them to find another one regardless of the cost in "money." Jesus told an enigmatic parable about this very subject one day to those who were "lovers of money." You will find it in Luke's Gospel, chapter 16. It is the story of the actions of a quite pragmatic and

138

unscrupulous "steward" (manager) in the world of the first century. It tells how a man caught cheating by his master went around to the master's creditors and created the impression that the master was a great benefactor. The result got the "steward" off the hook and gets a backhanded compliment from Jesus, who recommends the story to us with this punchline: "the sons of this world [Greek *age*] are more shrewd in dealing with their own generation than the sons of light" (Lk. 16:8 ESV).

Hank Rearden makes a mini-speech to Dagny at one point trying to say what he believes about wealth and luxury:

> "I've never despised luxury," he said, "yet I've always despised those who enjoyed it. I looked at what they called their pleasures and it seemed so miserably senseless to me—after what I felt at the mills. I used to watch steel being poured, tons of liquid steel running as I wanted it to, where I wanted it. And then I'd go to a banquet and I'd see people who sat trembling in awe before their own gold dishes and lace tablecloths, as if their dining room were the master and they were just objects serving it, objects created by their diamond shirt studs and necklaces, not the other way around. Then I'd run to the site of the first slag heap I could find— and they'd say that I didn't know how to enjoy life, because I cared for nothing but business." He looked at the dim, sculptured beauty of the room and at the people who sat at the tables. They sat in a manner of self-conscious display, as if the enormous cost of their clothes and the enormous care of their grooming should have fused into splendor, but didn't. Their faces had a look of rancorous anxiety.
> "Dagny, look at those people. They're supposed to be the playboys of life; the amusement-seekers and luxury-lovers. They sit there, waiting for this place to give them meaning, not the other way around. But they're always shown to us as the enjoyers of material pleasures—and then we're taught that enjoyment of material pleasures is evil. Enjoyment? Are they enjoying it? Is there some sort of perversion in what we're taught, some error that's vicious and very important?"
> "Yes, Hank—very vicious and very, very important." (p. 372)

At many points the characters of *Atlas Shrugged* are like the "dishonest manager"—wiser than many Christians know.

Chapter 13 - I Am; Therefore I Think

In order to grasp what premise drives Rand's hostility to Christian presuppositions as a basis for her philosophical ethics, it is necessary to take a brief gallop through the key traditions she was opposing, and a couple that she affirmed. This survey will hit only the high points, and especially a few that she would have considered "low points."

A Greek Tragedy

The Western tradition certainly goes back to the philosophical tradition of the Greeks, beginning with the Milesian pre-Socratic philosophers such as Thales, Anaximander, and Anaximenes. These were men who sought answers to the deep questions of life not in religious speculation, but in an effort to understand the world on its own terms. Their attempts to identify the basic elements of the universe (earth, air, fire, water) and to organize them hierarchically seems remarkably simplistic to us in our day, but they represent a real attempt to get beyond the fickle and immoral deities of the Greek religious tradition. They represent the first Western thinkers to attempt an application of "rationality" to our understanding of the natural world and the world of human beings.

The Greek philosophical tradition reached a high mark with Socrates, Plato, and Aristotle in the fifth and fourth centuries BC. Plato was the disciple of Socrates and ostensibly reflects the older man's views in his thirty-five publications, cast mainly in the form of Socratic dialogues. Several points are relevant to our discussion of Rand. First, Plato believed in the existence of "The Forms," as "eternal, changeless, and incorporeal" entities that "exist independently of thought."[44] These Forms exist in a higher realm than that of nature and they can only be encountered by us through *thought*. But for all those qualifications, they are no less real and were perceived by humans in their pre-born (eternal) existence as souls, and are more real than the world in which we live today, a world that is a

---

[44] Richard Kraut, "Plato," in *The Cambridge Dictionary of Philosophy*, 2nd ed., Robert Audi, gen. ed. (Cambridge: Cambridge University Press, 1999), 710.

shadowy reflection of the true Forms. Here are the true forms of all physically existing things in the world of nature, as well as the true forms of such ideals as justice, truth, and beauty. Hence for Plato, the most truly real world is not the world in which we eke out our lives, but another realm, above nature.

The only way to know and understand that world is to be challenged to perceive it by one who has already done so. In the Myth of the Cave (related in his political work, *Republic*) Plato writes of people who are chained to a wall in the bottom chamber of a cave deep in the earth. A fire is burning farther up inside the cave. Only capable of seeing the back wall of the cave, these chained persons do not see the world as it really is, a shadowy reflection of the real world of the Forms, but only see what they see. One of the prisoners is able to free himself and journeys up the cave to the outside world where he perceives the real world as it actually is. Deciding to tell his fellow prisoners, he descends back into the depths and relates what he has seen, in all its beauty contrasted to the drabness and unreality of their own world. But they do not believe him, and seek instead to kill him. This is the philosopher, the one who truly knows, and is a parable of Socrates, whom the men of Athens had condemned to death in AD 399.

In *Republic*, Plato calls for a regimented society, divided among the Bronze (farmers, craftsmen, builders), the Silver (soldiers and other lower-level administrators), and the Gold (the philosopher rulers). These three classes also correspond to the three elements of the human condition: appetites for food and sex, assertiveness that enables one to do brave and competitive tasks, and those who are guided above all by reason. ("The city is the man.") It needs to be understood that what Plato means by *reason* here is the ability to discern the Forms and to be guided then by impassionate application of the forms of justice, truth, and beauty to the task of ruling. Since the task of ruling is onerous, these Philosopher-Kings (or Queens, Plato was not distracted by gender) must be forced to rule, for the good of the collective.[45] Furthermore, they will not do any manual labor, as that is reserved for the Bronze class; in Plato's Greek culture manual

---

[45] Plato, *Republic, Complete Works*. John M. Cooper and D. S. Hutchinson, eds. (Indianapolis: Hackett, 1997), 7.5.

labor for "gentlemen" was universally loathed. Private property is eliminated in this most just society, and class distinctions are strictly regulated. Children are removed from their parents upon being weaned and are raised by state employees who are naturally suited to such tasks, and sex has as its only function the procreation that is needed for society to continue, though certainly the Bronze class will violate this principle since they are often governed by irrational passions.[46] Plato's theory imagines a planned and enforced structure of government for "the good of the people" that brooks no alteration and that allows for no freedom outside the structure.[47]

In his later years Plato took on a student from Stagira named Aristotle, who mentored under the older man for twenty years. Aristotle's mature philosophy shows some signs of agreement with Plato, but also many areas of disagreement. Following Plato's death in 347 BC, Aristotle traveled to Assos and Lesbos where he studied biology and gathered a good deal of biological information.[48] Aristotle came to disagree with Plato on the independent existence of the Forms, preferring to believe that these "Forms" existed only in the mind of the thinker. A famous painting of the two men by Raphael shows Plato pointing up to the heavens, while Aristotle's hand is stretched out horizontally, probably a reference to his moderate notion of the Golden Mean, but also an indication of his rejection of the metaphysical existence of the Forms. Philosophy has to do with this world, for Aristotle, not some imaginary spiritual realm.

For our purposes we will briefly examine Aristotle's Law of Non-Contradiction, his understanding of the Excluded Middle, and his Law of Identity, since these make up the section titles of *Atlas Shrugged*. These constitute Aristotle's exposition of the laws of thought, but they are "not merely how we must think in order to obtain knowledge; they also describe the fundamental

---

[46] Plato, *Republic*, 2.3-3.4.

[47] Plato, *Republic*, 3.4, 4.8, and throughout. See discussion in W. K. C. Guthrie, *A History of Greek Philosophy: IV. Plato: The Man and His Dialogues, Earlier Period* (Cambridge: Cambridge University Press, 1975), 434-68.

[48] Richard McKeon, *Introduction to Aristotle*, 2nd ed. (Chicago: University of Chicago Press, 1973), xii-xiii.

character of reality."[49] Aristotle stated the Law of Non-Contradiction in this way: "Nothing can both be and not be at the same time in the same respect." Something either is or it is not. And if it is, it is knowable by human thinking and experience. As Rand often said, "Nature, to be commanded, must be obeyed." This was one of Aristotle's most basic insights, and shows his dissatisfaction with Plato, who believed that what we perceive in this world is but a shadow of the Forms in the other realm, the true world. For Aristotle, this is the world of knowledge, and it is what it is.

The Principle of the Excluded Middle can easily be stated: "Either there is a tree over 500 feet tall or it is not the case that there is such a tree."[50] Aristotle famously gave the example of a sea battle. Either there will be a sea battle tomorrow or there will not be. There is no other option. Something either exists or does not exist at a given point in time and in some respect. The fact of what is there determines our response to it. The Law of Identity ("A is A") tells us that something is what it is at a given place and time. It cannot be something it is not. All of this is to say that what we experience in this world cannot both be and not be at the same time and in the same respect, that either it does or does not exist at some given place and time, and that it cannot be what it is not. For Aristotle, this entailed the notion that "the universe makes sense."[51] The fact that we are conscious and cognitively aware of this universe also makes it clear that our experience of the rational universe is understandable, since as John Galt says, "If nothing exists, then there can be no consciousness." (p. 1015)

It is this characteristic that constitutes "benevolence" for Rand. For Rand, the modern Aristotelian, these beliefs drive us to the conclusion that the world we have is what we have, and it is what it is. We might wish things were different, but they are not. We cannot live in a world of make-believe. In

---

[49] Douglas B. Rasmussen, "The Aristotelian Significance of the Section Titles of *Atlas Shrugged*: A Brief Consideration of Rand's View of Logic and Reality," in Younkins, ed., *Ayn Rand's* Atlas Shrugged, 34.

[50] Richard Purtill, "Principle of Excluded Middle," in Audi, ed., *Cambridge Dictionary of Philosophy*, 738.

[51] Rasmussen, "Aristotelian Significance," 35.

addition, since we are creatures dwelling in this material world, the world must be seen as good. This especially includes its material structures, structures that can be understood by the rational mind, as long as it maintains its focus on the Law of Non-Contradiction and the Principles of Either-Or and A is A. So, her heroes are copper miners, steel makers, railroad builders, and engineers. No Platonic pointing to the sky, this is a world of reality.

Aristotle's *Politics* is also crucial in understanding Rand. In Homer's *Iliad* we find the classic portrayal of Greek governance. Before the Gates of Troy, the Greeks are deciding whether to continue their ten-year-long war with the Trojans, or to go home defeated.[52] Achilles has gone to his tent, angry with King Agamemnon, and the King (*basileus* in Greek) now calls on the men to follow him. Learning of Achilles's reticence, the men (*ekklesia*, or "Assembly" in Greek) vote with their feet and rush to the ships. Odysseus quickly calls the Council (*boulé*, in Greek) together and urges the members to follow the king, at which time they call the men (*ekklesia*) back to the battle. This three-fold partition of governance between *basileus* (or, sometimes, *archon*, "ruler"), *boulé*, and *ekklesia* carries over into the governance of the later Greek city-states (singular, *polis*, plural, *poleis*), though the manner in which the three estates related to one another was diverse.

Aristotle discusses this in Books III and IV of his *Politics*.[53] He shows that the partition can be done badly or well. So, if an *ekklesia* attempts to rule without an active *boulé* or without an assertive *archon*, the result is "Pure Democracy," which can devolve into the kind of "mob-ocracy" that demanded (and got) the death of Socrates. If there is a powerful *boulé* without a substantial Assembly of the men of the *polis*, you wind up with an Oligarchy of the rich and powerful, such as prevailed at Sparta, and as we know, everyone hates the

---

[52] Homer, *The Iliad*, Samuel Butler, trans. (CreateSpace, 2010), Book 2.

[53] For a condensed version of this, see McKeon, *Introduction to Aristotle*, 592-659. For the complete text, see Aristotle, *The Politics and the Constitutions of Athens*, Cambridge Texts in the History of Political Thought, Stephen Everson, ed. (Cambridge: Cambridge University Press, 1996), 61-118).

Spartans (except the Spartans). Or, if you have an *archon* (or *basileus*) that bypasses the *boulé*, or worse, has them exterminated, you wind up with what Aristotle called a Tyranny (something that happened in various *poleis* throughout the Classic Age in Greece), the absolute rule of one over the subjugated masses with no intervening Council to limit his authority. On the other hand, if there is a healthy balance between the three estates, such as in a Monarchy (with a strong Council and involved Assembly), an Aristocracy (not merely based on land and money and that involves a strong First Citizen and on a voting Assembly), or a Polity (where the citizens have a voice, but where a Council is representative of them), there exists a much better possibility of a *just* political order. This is all in keeping with Aristotle's notion of the Golden Mean, where everything political and ethical must be done in moderation.

All of this is completely contrary to Plato's model of a Statist government with a ruling elite dominating the less fortunate and using a police force to keep them from rebellion. Aristotle believed that governments should flow naturally from the kind of topography and from the will of the people. He believed the greatest amount of justice in society would be found when governments balanced out the three estates, with none overly dominant and none absent.

Christian Thinkers and Mystics

For the first 280 or so years after its inception, Christianity labored under the tag of "illegal religion." But in AD 312 Constantine changed all of that by passing the Edict of Milan, legitimizing the faith. In 384 Emperor Theodosius made Christianity the religion of the empire, later outlawing paganism. The time for Christian emperors had come, and though this was a short-lived experience in the Roman West (the empire collapsed in 476), East Rome in Constantinople would witness centuries of Christian rule.

Augustine (d. 430) was dubious about the possibility for righteous governing in this age, even if the rulers were Christians, and he wrote extensively about that in his great work, *The City of God*. Augustine did, however, believe that *theology* was a *rational* exercise, and he developed the first full-blown theology that was both biblical and rational. He wrote, "Heaven forbid that God should hate in us that by which he made us superior to the animals! Heaven forbid that we should believe in such a way as not to accept or seek reasons, since we could not even believe if we did not possess rational souls."[54]

Reason also had an important place in the knowledge of God, though it must be conjoined with faith. We must combine the two, faith "that works by love" and understanding, "that He may be known more clearly and so loved more fervently."[55] For this West African church father, reason was a tool given by God to humans and was one aspect of the image of God in man, contrary to the premise of Galt and Rand. Augustine also believed in the Platonic Forms, but saw them as existing in the mind of the almighty and rational God who had created us. Augustine's thought was also mystical or pietistic in that he saw all of life as lived *coram deo*, in the presence of God; his autobiographical *Confessions* was one long prayer. His pietism, however, did not negate his emphasis on the importance of *reason*, nor did it result in him simply playing ideas off on one another in a fruitless effort to arrive at answers to any substantial questions. He believed that language could be used to predicate truths about both God and the world, and that both of these kinds of predications were central to what it means to be human.

Contemporary with Augustine was a group of Greek Eastern theologians who would establish a theological tradition quite different from that in the Latin West. Gregory of Nazianzus, Gregory of Nyssa, and Basil of Caesarea, the so-called Cappadocian Fathers, established a theological tradition in which predicating positive attributes of God was nearly impossible. Basil put it like this: "It is by His energies that we can say we know our God; we do not assert that we can come near to the essence itself, for His energies descend to us, but His essence remains unapproachable."[56] Gregory of Nyssa was even more emphatic, claiming, "The negative way of the knowledge of God is an ascendant undertaking of the mind that progressively eliminates all positive attributes of the object it wishes to

---

[54] Quoted in Rodney Stark, *The Victory of Reason: How Christianity Led to Freedom, Capitalism, and Western Success* (New York: Random House, 2005), 7.

[55] Augustine, *The Trinity*, Stephen McKenna, trans. (New York: Catholic University Press of America, 1963), 8.9.13.

[56] Quoted in Vladimir Lossky, *The Mystical Theology of the Eastern Church* (Crestwood, NY: St. Vladimir's Seminary Press, 1976), 72.

146

attain, in order to culminate finally in a kind of apprehension by supreme ignorance of Him who cannot be an object of knowledge. We can say that it is an intellectual experience of the mind's failure when confronted with something beyond the conceivable."[57] Then there is this from Maximus the Confessor, writing about three hundred years after the Cappadocians, "Negative statements about divine matters are the only true ones."[58] Reason had little role to play in formulating an understanding of God. This is essentially the understanding of John Galt as to the Christian conception of God, as we quoted him above.

In keeping with this view of knowledge, Eastern Christianity has virtually eschewed any attempt to formulate a systematic theology.[59] "The great mysteries of the faith are for the East matters of adoration rather than analysis."[60] There is simply nothing in Orthodox Catholicism like Thomas Aquinas's *Summa Theologiae*, Calvin's *Institutes*, or Barth's *Church Dogmatics*. The net effect of this perspective is that Orthodox Catholicism devolves immediately to *mysticism* as the highest expression of the faith, with no concomitant concern to give *rational* expression to theology alongside of faith in the way that Augustine and later Western thinkers would do.

Enter Thomas Aquinas. In the 1220's a group of Muslim, Latin, and Jewish scholars came together in the city of Toledo and in an amazing demonstration of scholarly *camaraderie*, translated many of the works of Aristotle into Latin that had previously been available only in Greek and Arabic.[61] This joint effort ought to be seen as "an acute source of embarrassment"[62] for many

---

[57] Cited in Vladimir Lossky, "Apophasis and Trinitarian Theology," in Vladimir Lossky, *In the Image and Likeness of God* (Crestwood, NY: St. Vladimir's Seminary Press, 1974), 13.

[58] Maximus the Confessor, *Book of Ambiguities*, 20, cited in Jaroslav Pelikan, *The Spirit of Eastern Christendom* (600-1700) (Chicago: University of Chicago Press, 1974), 32-33.

[59] The one exception is John of Damascus's (d. 754) *Exposition of the Orthodox Faith*.

[60] Daniel B. Clendenin, *Eastern Orthodox Christianity: A Western Perspective* (Grand Rapids: Baker, 1994), 53.

[61] Richard Rubenstein, *Aristotle's Children: How Christians, Muslims and Jews Discovered Ancient Wisdom and Illuminated the Middle Ages* (New York: Harvest, 2004), 15.

[62] Rubenstein, *Aristotle's Children*, 9.

147

modernists, who believe that in this period of the "Dark Ages" that only prejudice, ignorance, and intolerance were the hallmarks of the day. These translations of Aristotle into Latin would become the foundation for a new scholastic movement in the newly formed Western universities, such as Paris, Oxford, Cambridge and Bologna, and would render Aristotle's insights into logic, metaphysics, epistemology, and other areas of knowledge available once again to educated persons. Thomas Aquinas (1225-74) would incorporate these insights into his new scholastic theology. Thomas offered insights into the doctrines of God, salvation, the church, and many other areas of traditional theological *loci*, but his rational theology also explored the realms of politics, economics, psychology, and other realms that went beyond traditional Western themes, and that certainly went far beyond the limited spheres of exploration in Eastern Orthodox thought.

The kingdom of Russia converted to Christianity in AD 989. Queen Olga witnessed a high mass in the basilica of Hagia Sophia in Constantinople, the largest church in the world at the time and one decorated all round with magnificent stained glass windows. Stunned, she exclaimed that only God could dwell in such a place, and the whole kingdom subsequently went over to the Orthodox faith. When the Byzantine Empire later fell to the Ottoman Turks in 1453, "the main centers of eastern Christian thought shifted to Russia, and especially the cities of Kiev and Moscow."[63] Writers such as A. S. Khomyakov (d. 1860) and Vladimir Soloviev (d. 1900) "did much to develop the intellectual foundations of Russian Orthodox theology during the nineteenth century,"[64] and they did so in keeping with the mystical, anti-rational manner passed on to them by the Orthodox Catholicism in whose heritage they stood. So, the faith of the Church in which Rand was raised was just that—an anti-rational, mystical faith, and one that had no answers to offer when Marxist Communism swept the country after 1917.

A new chapter in the history of the West would be written after AD 1517. In that year a Catholic professor of Bible in Saxony initiated a debate over various

---

[63] Alister E. McGrath, *Historical Theology: An Introduction to the History of Christian Thought* (Oxford: Blackwell, 1998), 241.

[64] McGrath, *Historical Theology*, 241.

doctrinal aberrations (in his opinion) that would mushroom in just a few years into a theological and ecclesiastical revolution that we now call the Reformation. One of the key second generation figures of that revolt, John Calvin, would go on to build on insights from Augustine and Thomas Aquinas to formulate a new rational theology. That theology, like Augustine's, would fuse rationalism and piety, and would go even farther (and would be a more biblical corrective) than Thomas in articulating a foundation for politics (even the basis for political rebellion), economics, and social life. This theology would also serve as a foundational ideology for a significant segment of settlers in the new world of America in the seventeenth century.[65]

Enlightenment and Modernity: Smart and Smarter?

In the sixteenth century in the West, new formulations of science and philosophy would bring about a revolution both in the intellectual world and in the world in general. Francis Bacon (d. 1626) was the father of empiricism and established the *inductive method* as the true way to conduct scientific enquiry. His work was quite controversial since it overturned previous "science" that had been based on Aristotelian speculations.[66] But it laid the foundations upon which Galileo, Newton, Brahe, Boyle and others would build. This new science was not merely *technology*. "Science is a *method* utilized in *organized* efforts to formulate *explanations of nature*, always subject to modifications and correction through *systematic observation*."[67] That is, science consists of two components, theory and research.[68] It is important to note that science was created in one place, the West, only one time, though it had been on the way to formulation for centuries, but again, only in the West.[69] Western Christian thinkers such as William of Occam and Nicolas of Cusa had been formulating, bit by bit, observations of nature that

---

[65] See, for instance, David W. Hall, *Calvin in the Public Square: Liberal Democracies, Rights, and Civil Liberties* (Philipsburg, NJ: P & R, 2009).

[66] Aristotle, for all his greatness in the areas of logic and metaphysics, was no empirical scientist.

[67] Stark, *Victory of Reason*, 12, italics in original.

[68] Stark, *Victory of Reason*, 12.

eventually coalesced into Bacon's great insights. "Real science arose only once: in Europe."[70] China, Greece, and Islam all had alchemy, but only in Europe did that develop into chemistry. Why? Because only Christianity, and really only Western Christianity, had a rational God who could be known, and whose thoughts could be "thought after him," to use the famous phrase of Tycho Brahe. As we have seen, not even Eastern Orthodoxy, the Christianity of Greece and Russia, had the intellectual apparatus to make that jump. But the religious tradition of Augustine, Thomas Aquinas, and John Calvin did.[71]

The Enlightenment brought us modern natural science, but that is not all it brought. It brought the philosophical explorations of René Descartes. Descartes (d. 1650) lived most of his adult life in the shadow of the Thirty Years' War (1618-48), a war fought between Catholics and Protestants over what was the correct interpretation of Christianity.[72] This created in Descartes an epistemological crisis. If equally committed Christians cannot decide what is really true (the Catholic or the Protestant version) and if that disagreement leads inevitably to a horrendous war (and this war *was* horrendous), how can we know anything for certain? Descartes's project began with radical doubt. What can I doubt about my own experience? Well, I can doubt almost everything about my experience. After all, perhaps I am just a brain in a vat and an evil genie (we would say a "mad scientist") is feeding sense data to me by tubes and wires.[73] But there is one thing I cannot doubt: that I am doubting. From this observation Descartes formulating the *cogito ergo sum*, "I think, therefore I am." But in so doing he posited a dualism between mind and body. Only the mind can formulate the certainty of the body's existence. Along the way he also made the knowing subject, not the external physical world, the arbiter of truth. In this he became one

---

[69] Rodney Stark, *The Triumph of Christianity: How the Jesus Movement Became the World's Largest Religion* (New York: HarperOne, 2011), 279.

[70] Stark, *Victory of Reason*, 14.

[71] See the excellent discussion of this in Nancy R. Pearcey and Charles B. Thaxton, *The Soul of Science: Christian Faith and Natural Philosophy* (Wheaton: Crossway, 1994).

[72] Peter W. Wilson, *The Thirty Years War: Europe's Tragedy* (Cambridge: Belknap, 2011).

of the chief architects for modernity (and to an extent, even post-modernity), the belief that all truth is subject to my formulation of it.

If Descartes was the philosophical architect for modernity, Immanuel Kant was its destroyer. Kant read Descartes through the lens of Scottish philosopher David Hume. Hume had argued that we can never have any knowledge of metaphysical realities. We cannot, for instance, establish *causation*. I may observe that when a billiard ball strikes another, that the one that is struck then moves in a certain way. But Hume argued that we cannot make a logical case for causation in this event, only constant conjunction, since cause is a *metaphysical*, not a *physical*, conclusion.[74] Kant's project led him to propose that reality is divided into two realms, the noumenal and the phenomenal. The phenomenal world is the world of our experience, of rocks, babies, and Volkswagens (not in Kant's day, of course). We have been created (Kant believed in God, unlike Hume) to experience this world by means of "*a priori categories* of cognition," such as number, distance, time, color, etc. These categories of cognition enable us to parse our world and to communicate with other sentient creatures about it. The noumenal world (the metaphysical world), which includes knowledge of causation, along with angels and God, is unavailable to our cognition. We can believe in that world, but we cannot know it.[75]

Kant, like Descartes, had bifurcated reality into two realms. Descartes had divided between mind and body and Kant had bifurcated between the world of experience and the world of true meaning and knowledge, with the clear implication that the most important of these realms is unavailable to us.[76] Note also the similarities between these thinkers and the earlier Plato, for whom the Forms constituted the real reality while this world is only shadows and shades.

---

[73] René Descartes, *A Discourse on Method and Meditations on First Philosophy*, Donald Cress, trans. (New York: Hackett, 1993.

[74] Colin Brown, *Christianity & Western Thought: A History of Philosophers, Ideas & Movements*, vol. 1: From the Ancient World to the Age of Enlightenment (Downers Grove: InterVarsity, 1990), 235-58.

[75] Brown, *Christianity & Western Thought*, 309-29.

Think also of the similarity in all of these forms of "dualism" with Greek and Russian Orthodox theology, for whom God and even ultimate reality are merely things we can *contemplate*, but not *know*.

Super State and Super Man

It remains only to discuss Marx and Nietzsche to complete our preparation for understanding and critiquing Rand. Karl Marx was born to a Jewish family in Prussia in 1818, a family that had converted to Lutheranism in part to advance his father's career as a lawyer. He studied philosophy in Berlin, eventually receiving a doctor's degree (from Jena) and then proceeded to become a writer, editing a left-wing political periodical in Prussia, but censorship issues there drove him first to Paris and several other cities, eventually landing him in London, where he would live out his life.

Marx is in many ways the *opposite* of Adam Smith, the philosopher from Scotland who had articulated the basic intellectual structure of free market economics in the previous century. The Scotsman had argued that when every man pursues his own self-interests, "this would result in an outcome beneficial to all, whereas Marx argued that the pursuit of self-interest would lead to anarchy, crisis, and the dissolution of the property-based system itself."[77] Smith had a generally positive outlook on the human condition if only governments would honor man's "natural liberty"; Marx believed all governments were corrupt and oppressive. Smith believed that the "invisible hand" would boost everyone along and raise all ships, while Marx believed that the "iron fist of competition" would pulverize workers, even while it enriched those who owned the means of production.

In 1848 he met Friedrich Engels in Paris and the two men wrote the pamphlet, *The Communist Manifesto*. Later, in London, he would pursue the work that he dreamed of writing, *Das Kapital*, or, in English, just *Capital*. Marx believed that in economics, being human involves an effort at changing the world

---

[76] It should be noted that Scottish Common Sense Realism offered a corrective to the Kantian "solution." Brown, *Christianity & Western Thought*, 259-279.

[77] Sylvia Nasar, *Grand Pursuit: The Story of Economic Genius* (New York: Simon and Schuster, 2011), 11-47.

around us by labor, and so, *labor* is crucial to what it means to be human. But older economic systems had robbed people of their ability to do that, especially the manorial system, which utilized other person's labor to bring wealth to the barons, the bishops, and a few others. *Capitalism* (this was Marx's term, which is why we use it here) was better in that it gave people some access to some goods and services needed for happiness, but Capitalism is only *quantitatively* better that Manorialism, not *qualitatively*. In the older system people had to turn over the produce of their farms to others, while in Capitalism people have to sell their labor for wages. Those who own the means of production, the *bourgeoisie*, employ workers to produce goods which are then sold for excess *profit*, profit that the owners keep for themselves. Profits were *inherently* unjust, in Marx's view, since the *owners* of the *means of production* did not generate them themselves.

Marx's economic theory was *materialistic* and deterministic. Marx had made a close study of the writings of Georg Hegel, a Berlin scholar who believed that history moved along a predictable and inevitable trajectory, always moving toward a higher consciousness (what Hegel called the *Geist*) and a more just and advanced social and political culture. Marx borrowed from Hegel, arguing that the Roman slavery system had collided with Feudalism, thus producing Capitalism, but that now Capitalism was headed for a conflict with the new Socialism, the outcome of which would be a new and more just system of political economy, Communism. Communism was the goal toward which history was aimed, but it had to pass first through Capitalism, then Socialism (what Marx saw as the developing conflict in his day) before utopia could be realized.[78]

What was this Socialism that Marx trumpeted? What must be done now (in 1848 when he wrote the *Manifesto*) so that a better world will one day dawn? He and Engels called for a ten-point program: abolition of private property, heavy progressive or graduated income tax, abolition of all right of inheritance, confiscation of property of emigrants, centralization of credit in the hands of the State, centralization of the means of communication and transport in the hands of

---

[78] Nasar, *Grand Pursuit*, 33-38.

the State, extension of factories and instruments of production owned by the State (along with reclamation of waste lands by the State), equal obligation of all to work, combination of agriculture with manufacturing industries and the gradual abolition of the distinction between town and country, and the free education of all children in public schools. All of this was to be increasingly placed under the direction of an authoritative Administrative State.

Marx also contended that Capitalism was inherently *class* based, and that these class barriers, like the ones from the Middle Ages, could not ultimately be breached. The proletariat (workers) would remain the proletariat while the bourgeoisie would remain entrenched in their protected perches, enjoying the privilege and luxury of generational profits. This was un-reform-able in Marx's view, and the intractableness of this fact would be the key to the eventual rise of Communism. *Class conflict* was one of the keys to future utopia, and focusing on such conflict in his writings was important to him in order to trumpet it to anyone who would hear him. Urging for class conflict to accelerate would be one of the keys to bringing about a just system.

Marx was not completely negative toward entrepreneurship. The Free Market system, in Marx's view, has the ability to be a very powerful economic system because it is constantly improving the means of production. It can do this because of the advances in technology and because it has so much surplus value to work with. Marx expected, though, that a crisis would come upon Capitalism when profits would eventually fall even as the economy was growing. One crisis would eventually become many separate crises, and the resulting trauma would in the end collapse the system when the proletariat, out of frustration, would eventually rise up and wrest the means of production from the hands of the bourgeoisie. "The worse things got, he reasoned, the better the odds of revolution." Marx and Engels argued that this eventuality was "inevitable." "Workers of the world, unite!" And unite they did in the world of Ayn Rand's childhood. What caused her such frustration as she came to understand the USA to which she migrated was the apparent rapid drift of her new homeland toward the tragedy she had left behind.

We note, finally, in this intellectual primer the importance of Nietzsche to *Atlas Shrugged*. Like Marx, he was a Prussian. Also like Marx, he was an atheist, and a particularly virulent one. He was also an advocate of the idea that each generation produces a very small group of truly remarkable men, and that these men should be allowed unfettered access to the means that will display their greatness, unhindered by government or religion. He harked back to the figure of Prometheus as an example of that. He thought of that figure, who gave fire to humankind, as a "titanically striving individual," who through a sacrilegious act of defiance against divine authority, makes "the sublime idea of active sin . . . the truly Promethean virtue."[79] Rand was influenced by the cult surrounding Prometheus, and especially Nietzsche's version of it, and key figures in the novel are clearly modeled after this. At one point in her philosophical pilgrimage she adhered to a more elitist take on her heroic figures—that is, that the masses of humanity could not be expected to achieve a rational existence like the Nietzschean *Ubermensch*. After she came to America and became involved in democratic politics, she became persuaded that there was a vast middle ground of those who were not the few who could influence the entire context of civilization for good, but neither were they mere pawns to be manipulated by the muscle men at the other extreme—men and women she saw as millionaires in cahoots with political looters. In other words, she came to trust the institutions of American democracy, but *Atlas Shrugged* is a loud warning about a course she saw as in progress and inimical to democratic capitalism.

---

[79] Friedrich Nietzsche, *The Birth of Tragedy*, Michael Tanner, ed., Shaun Whiteside, trans. (New York: Harmondsworth, 1993). We are indebted to Kirsti Mensaas, "Ayn Rand's recasting of Ancient Myths," in *Ayn Rand's Atlas Shrugged*, 133, for this citation.

Chapter 14 - Who Is Jesus Christ?

Ayn Rand consciously cast herself as opposed to religion, especially Christianity for two reasons: "it established unrealizable, abstract ethical ideas that made men cynical when they fell short,[80] and its emphasis on faith denied reason."[81] Further, she said of Christianity that it "is the best kindergarten of communism possible."[82] It was this conviction that led her to seek out an "ethics of individualism" that did not require the sanction of Christianity. She mused in her journal entries during the Thirties about the nature of man in the Nietzschean mold (as we have discussed it above) and his ability to achieve complete mastery of his emotional makeup through reason, thus becoming truly man as he should and must be to live with reality. Could such a man arrive at an acceptable ethical system that was primarily individual and naturalistic, or was ethics only to be achieved as a social conception and derived in some degree at least from Christianity (in the sense of coming from God)? Could the tendency to emotional rather than rational processes (generally contradictory rather than harmonic) be seen as a "form of undeveloped reason, a form of stupidity?"[83] Rand was not the first, nor will she be the last to wrestle with the nature of man in Adam as the Bible presents him. John Galt rejected the biblical construct in his speech as absurd and insulting because it required a mystical faith that required one to posit another reality with which one could not truly grapple directly by means of cognitive ability. "Original Sin" was supposed to be the acquiring of cognitive ability, rationality, the ability to think. The concomitant parts of the new reality were work and creativity and sexuality. These things make man (and woman) human, what he and she are in the reality that can be known to reason. In the Randian system this cannot be "sin," some fatal flaw, since to be in this state is to

---

[80] There is no evidence in her writings and journals that she ever considered the Pauline discussion of this dilemma in Romans 6-8.

[81] Burns, *Goddess*, 29. This despite the fact she saw *The Fountainhead* as "a defense of egoism in its real meaning, egoism as a new faith," Burns, 41.

[82] Ibid., 43.

[83] Ibid., 29.

find only death, not life. To attempt to live in this current reality of rational "benevolence" on the basis of premises gleaned from a mystical "reality" is to court death as the only end of such existence. It is, therefore, a morality of death. At least she was dead-on in part of that conclusion. One must determine the nature of reality to live in it, rather than to die in it. Aristotle's three propositions rule in any rational universe.

Hugh Akston taught his three brilliant students and admonished Dagny Taggart at one point (or more) that when your formulations don't fit reality you should "check your premises." According to this philosophical axiom it is not evil to be mistaken in knowledge. Evil is the willful attempt to fake reality and seek to convince others of the validity of such humbug. But just suppose the premise of "original sin" does in fact explain reality as we rationally apprehend it. What then? How shall we explain man as self-destructive and apparently incorrigible when it comes to reason? More to the point, what if reality has been altered by the very presence of this flaw in Man? What if the "benevolence" Rand saw in the universe is not just that it is rational, but that it is designed by a Creator who wishes to be "found" or better, "finds" us? If the universe is rational and man is capable of reasoned and accurate inference from the knowledge base available to him,[84] what accounts for death in an otherwise life-oriented system? Rand's system in effect says that all of life is a struggle, and if one does not reach the pinnacle of aspiration before death, the struggle itself is worth the trouble. That really isn't far from the street philosophy: Life is tough and then you die!

We would submit that contrary to John Galt the real culture, morality of death is the objectivist one of Ayn Rand, for it cannot account for death itself in the current reality, and worse, it cannot posit a way out of death into life. The best it can offer is the amelioration of present circumstances toward a "better" existence materially, culturally, and politically, but it does not change the context of death. It remains true, "It is appointed for man to die once" (Heb 9:27 ESV), not only as an axiom of Christian Scripture but undeniably as a datum of simple

---

[84] Not that man is capable of exhaustive knowledge, but that he is capable of accurate knowledge.

observation in human reality.[85] One does not need a received text to know this as an Aristotelian premise. But one can also argue from some observed phenomena that this reality produces violence toward the innocent and among the would-be dominators in world history. World literary documents from ancient times to the present show men and women vying for supremacy, not of the mind but of the physical realm of existence, with the outlier possibility that immortality will somehow follow. They do not seek to persuade so much as they plot and threaten and murder and otherwise do violence individually and corporately, and they do it regardless of the manner in which they are repeating the folly of the past, to which they are privy. They accumulate knowledge, but it does not lead to the cessation of violence and fraud. They simply become more sophisticated in its application, such that the twentieth century was the most destructive of human life by human beings in the history of the planet. The culture and morality of death reach into the womb for millions of victims and into the retirement communities of the elderly and the hospitals of the supposed "healers" and commit murder for the sake of convenience and the avoidance of the costs of prolonging life. What claims to be about improving the "quality of life" has death as its tool and goal.

The category of "stupidity" does not fit such a climax to the age of "enlightenment" and "reason." The term "evil" fits very well. We would propose that mankind has "reasoned" that death awaits everyone anyway, so what difference does it make if some die prematurely by violence so that the lot of others, particularly the "others" to which we are attached and committed, is improved. Or, as in the case of the myths of ancient legend and epic poetry, wouldn't it be better if one might die in a heroic struggle rather than supine submission to either fate or the "will of the gods." The Bible has just such a story in its early chapters. Genesis 5 records the apparent death by natural causes of a number of long-lived descendants of Adam. It then records in the beginning of the

---

[85] We use the Bible in our references throughout this section not as the coercive tool Rand saw it to be but as the narrative presented as a "revelation" of the reality behind the phenomena of our sensory observations. The rational question is whether this text(s) presents a better formulation of reality than the non-theistic formulation of objectivism. In any case both Rand and the Bible claim that failure to live up to the constructive picture of reality they paint has life and death consequences. Only in this sense are they both coercive.

sixth chapter that there were heroic figures who "took" as they wished from among their inferiors what appear to be "trophy wives"[86] and assumed the position of "giants" and/or "heroes."[87] Then the comment is made that God saw into the heart of mankind and noted that the entirety of his inner considerations and commitments was "only evil continually." Ultimately a flood of cataclysmic dimensions destroys everything but one family of 8 people. They find "grace" in the eyes and dealings of God with them and survive. Out of this experience comes the biblical maxim called the *lex talionis*, a concept that evil must be curbed and punished by the hand of man standing in for God, and the punishment must fit the crime (Gen 9:6). Most commentators believe this is the foundation of governments among men that supersedes the rule of "heroic" despots and petty chieftains.

This story also asserts another factor that mitigates against the incorrigible inner propensity and devising of evil "continually"—man is created in the "image of God," the reason man's blood should be "shed" in legal punishment. To summarize the early biblical picture, man has been created in the image of God, but no matter how long he lives (even a thousand years?) he doesn't get it right and degenerates into violence such that a divine judgment is necessary, but "grace" continues the story by rescuing some out of the cataclysm of the flood. What has led to this reality? It is what Galt labeled and theologians have called "original sin"—the fact that man has "fallen" from an original state of innocence into a state of exile from the pristine conditions into which he was first placed and the fellowship he had with his creator. What was that sin? Well, it was not the acquisition of reason and intellect, the ability to think for himself. He had that as part of the image of God. It was not sexuality, for the creator saw him as man alone and said "Not good!" and "built" him a "helper" of "corresponding" attributes to facilitate their becoming "one flesh." It was not the ability to do creative "work," for that was part of his commission in the Garden. What then

---

[86] A term coined by Thorstein Veblen in a previous century.

was the first sin? It was seeking to be autonomous in a specific way—"the knowledge of good and evil." It was not merely seeking to understand and know what good and evil is about. It was seeking this knowledge apart from the discovery of it in fellowship with God. This clearly subordinates man to God with reference to differentiating morality, but in the context of Genesis it is also an overarching designation for the entire creative enterprise and what is intended for man in it. The book itself closes with the declaration of Joseph to his brothers, "You meant evil against me but God meant it for good" (Gen 50:20 ESV).

After the great flood we now see mankind in the light of two factors that are intended to explain his ongoing condition and experience: (1) He is created in the image of God (2) His inner intentions are continually evil. Nevertheless the world goes on and gradually the narrative unfolds revealing God's means of remedying this dichotomy. Rand was correct to posit that man must fight for a unity of nature against some force that constantly tears him apart. Nevertheless, as she asserts, it cannot be that man is separated in his essential nature. He IS a "living soul." He does not merely HAVE a soul, or spirit. His mind, his reason, his consciousness, his self is single, both physical and spiritual (in the sense of non-physical). This much she and Galt get right, but they do not take into account as serious the other possibility to explain why man is self-destructive and apparently inured to reason as an ethical and moral guide. What if the premise of "original sin" is correct. What if the entire universe is so geared in its essential nature that moral failing on the part of man sets it on a course of destruction? If, as the Genesis narrative claims, man was made the ruler of creation as the viceroy of God, is it not possible that within that framework of reality it makes sense that moral failing has consequences far beyond the mere "stupidity" of one pair? The biblical reality says that man's moral failing has put the whole creation out of joint so that not only is man throughout his generations corrupted, but the world has been turned into a place of toil and futility in the very thing the original pair were

---

[87] See *Seeking the City*, for a fuller exegesis of this passage and the flood narrative. We will not enter the debate on the historicity of these recorded events except that we take them to be representative of actual historical reality. For our purposes here, we are demonstrating that the biblical explanation of man's evil is a rational construct accounting for his behavior and the death that dogs his footsteps.

placed here to do. Paul put it this way on both counts: "in Adam all die" (1 Cor 15:22; cf. Rom 5:12), and "the creation was subjected to futility" (Rom 8:23). Furthermore, the Apostle Paul says that there is a reason for the apparent "stupidity" of men and women: "For although they knew God, they did not honor him as God or give thanks to him, but they became futile in their thinking, and their foolish hearts were darkened" (Rom 1:21 ESV).

We contend that this explanation of the condition of human life on this earth comports with the apprehension of it that comes from rational observation. Rand herself paints the characters who actually betray and (devilishly?) oppose the "men of the mind" as completely unsympathetic near-savages at times. They are brutish and ugly and worthy of overflowing disdain. In part this reflects Rand's experience in the Soviet system and the disdain she received in intellectually elitist circles of the left in this country. They seem to us to be far more than lacking in understanding or knowledge, and she does call them "evil." But from what does that evil stem? She would say they have been improperly taught and influenced by the descendants of shamans and witchdoctors who passed along a heritage of mysticism and superstition to the Medieval scholastics and Christian theologians. Without commending any theological framework beyond our previous analysis above, we suggest a check of premises. What if the biblical premise is correct and Rand's is short on knowledge? What is the answer?

Man needs more than an education and a reorientation to reason in his inner life. He needs what the Bible calls "salvation" from his condition and a renewal of the image of God along with the renewal of the entire Creation. Most of all, death must be abolished as a destination. How can this be accomplished? The biblical narrative points to Jesus Christ, the central figure of history, especially in his death and resurrection on this earth. The Old Testament anticipates his arrival by pointing again and again to the failure of humans and their institutions to set things right on earth. The New Testament reports the historical events surrounding his first entrance into and exit from our human situation and then goes on to interpret for us the meaning of those events. Throughout this explanation there is the continuing theme that he shall return to

161

finish what has begun in those events—the creation of "a new heavens and a new earth in which righteousness dwells" (2 Pet 3:13).

What is the meaning of his death and resurrection? It is the fulfillment of the ancient system of "sacrifice," perverted among the many nations of the world as attempts to placate and appease the gods with offerings that will win favor for family and business and empire, but carefully presented in the Old Testament as the satisfaction of justice for the sins of the nation and the personal confessions of the individual sinner. The victim, an animal, enters death in the place of the nation and the individual so the sinner(s) may continue to live and have fellowship with God, who, by the way, has no need of "offerings." These "sacrifices" by their very nature could not suffice to pay for the sins of people made in the image of God. One who is also in that image must come and offer himself as a spotless sacrifice, bearing away the wrath of God against sin and making a way for man to go on living in fellowship with God rather than descending forever into a pile of particles blowing on the wind. How does the Bible show us that the man crucified in the middle of a tri-partite execution somehow died a death that was different from the other two? The one in the middle came out of the grave three days later and was seen over a period of 40 days by several hundred witnesses on the earth and ascending through the skies to the heavenly realm. He was also seen and heard by three men in the heavenly realm—Stephen, Paul, and John the author of Revelation. Once again Paul gives the sense of what this means: this One was "declared to be the Son of God with power...by His resurrection from the dead" (lit., "from among dead people" Rom 1:4).[88] The meaning of this event is that what Jesus did satisfied the justice of God (Rom 3:23-26) and made possible the presentation of Jesus Christ as the Savior and Lord of sinners who come to Him in faith and follow Him in discipleship.

The narrative of Scripture has now come full circle from the creation of Man in the image of God as His creative delegated ruler of the earthly domain and

---

[88] For the most comprehensive scholarly presentation of the rational arguments and historical data supporting the historicity of the resurrection of Jesus see N. T. Wright, *The Resurrection of the Son of God* (Minneapolis: Augsberg, 2003).

162

the skies above, to the Fall into sin and curse and futility, to the failure of all attempts to set things right, to the arrival of another just like Adam but without sin (Negatively) and full of the Spirit and wisdom (positively), to the just sacrifice for sin and its acceptance by the Creator, to the promise of His return to finish the work of new creation. The moral nature of the universe has now been "righted" by the work of the true Man of God's choice. The question we ask here is what if this premise is true? How does one rule it out if it is not? It requires a rational process of assembling of data and interpretation of that data, a process Rand calls reason. No one is expected to simply accept the teaching of the church without rational assessment, but neither is it acceptable to simply dismiss it out of hand as an impossible construct in light of known reality. The question is, Who is Jesus Christ? Paul called him the "last Adam...the second man...the man of heaven" (1 Cor 15:45-49) whose mission is to infuse His Spirit into a new race of men and women who will be fit for the new creation that is coming. Thomas bowed to Him after the resurrection as he saw the wounds in his body and called Him "My Lord and My God" (Jn 20:28). Jesus Himself claimed "I am the way, and the truth, and the life. No one comes to the Father except through me" (Jn. 14:6). Simon Peter preached that "There is no other name under heaven given among men whereby we must be saved" (Acts 4:12). John wrote, affirming the connection between Jesus and life, "Whoever has the Son has life; whoever does not have the Son of God does not have life" (1 Jn. 5:12). C. S. Lewis put the Aristotelian proposition like this famously in his *Mere Christianity*:

> "I am trying here to prevent anyone saying the really foolish thing that people often say about Him: "I'm ready to accept Jesus as a great moral teacher, but I don't accept His claim to be God." That is the one thing we must not say. A man who said the sort of things Jesus said would not be a great moral teacher. He would either be a lunatic — on a level with the man who says he is a poached egg — or else he would be the Devil of Hell. You must make your choice. Either this man was, and is, the Son of God: or else a madman or something worse. You can shut Him up for a fool, you can spit at Him and kill Him as a demon; or you can fall at His feet and call Him Lord and God. But let us not come with any patronizing nonsense about His being a great human teacher. He has not left that open to us. He did not intend to."

To anyone who has spent any time studying objectivism and the works of Ayn Rand without the premise that the biblical narrative correctly assesses reality as we know it, we would offer this proposition. Give the same diligence to the study of the primary documents of Christianity found in the Bible. Read it through again and again as you have *Atlas Shrugged* or *The Fountainhead*. Check out the works of a great scholar like N. T. Wright who is not known as some kind of right-wing obscurantist but a seasoned observer of the world and a churchman and world-class biblical scholar. Read Rodney Stark, *Discovering God: The Origins of the Great Religions and the Evolution of Belief*, as an orientation to the current state of studies in comparative religion. Use the *Apologetics Bible* as a tool and study aid. Be sure to use a good translation like the *English Standard Version* or the *Holman Christian Standard Bible*. Do the spade-work of a Randian rationalist and assess the claims of the Bible against reality as you know it. Answer the question Jesus put to his disciples one day: He asked them first about the opinions of others, and then He put them on the spot—"Who do you say I am" (Mt. 16:15, 16). Answer it for yourself and make John Galt proud of your individualism. Who is Jesus Christ?

John Galt & the Christian Church

A final word is in order to the Christian taking time to consider *Atlas Shrugged* against the context of our time and the claims of Christ. The "altruism" against which Rand rebels in her characters is the essence of the true "hole" in the heart of today's Christendom. It is a mistaken refusal to live for the only "Other" that matters in the way that Christ did—as one who brings life to the dead and dying, not by *living for* them but living and dying completely in harmony with the will of His Father, with whom He was in complete agreement. He refused to live out the caricature of the God of Abraham, Isaac, and Jacob on offer in the Judaism(s)[89] of His day. He refused to conform to their folk religion, for it was the way of death. Only His was the way of Life. It is this sense in which John Galt refused to live out his life for the sake of another man. He would only sacrifice

---

[89] Modern scholarship is in substantial agreement that there was a spectrum of Jewish belief and practice that was not monolithic except in the affirmation of the One God and Israel's place in the scheme of history.

himself, his ego, in the service of those things that drove his own values (regardless of whether we agree with his values or not) which he saw as compatible with the life worthy to be lived. Jesus would not consent (or "sanction" in Galt's use of that term) to the conformity required of him by the authorities of Rome and Jerusalem so that he might go on living a life of sorts—a life lived at the point of a gun. No, He confronted that thing in the soul of Judaism (the kind that would come to dominate Jewish "religion") and Roman patronage and said, "Whom seek ye?" He conformed to the will of the Father, His only value in life that mattered to Him and said take me and let these around me go. And He did it because He and the Father were authors of the only plan that would lead to LIFE for both Himself and His followers. In this is LIFE for all who follow both His way and His words. Galt would say that this particular way is mistaken and unknowable, but he would also affirm that if it is real and knowable, nothing must be allowed to get in the way of attaining it (cf. Phi 3:12-14).

This is what the Apostle Paul is describing when he says to the Corinthians, "Death works in us, but life in you." Paul knew that he could conform to Corinthian expectations and live without controversy and within the approval and support of the congregation if he would only give in to what was becoming the folk religion of the Corinthian church. This he refused, pointedly, to do and made it a matter of the survival of the true Gospel. That was the hill Paul was willing to die on. He, like Christ before him and in him, clarified his values to the church and challenged them at the heart of their conformity to cultural expectations. He refused to become anti-Christ, approving their acquisition of Roman and Greek and Judaistic expectations, for this was the only way to LIFE for the church. He knew within himself that, whether he could see it happen before his eyes or not, LIFE would follow his death for the Gospel of the cross for which he felt no shame (2 Cor 4:11).

The modern church needs the same leadership from its pastors and teachers and elders and deacons today. It needs some who will learn from John Galt as they seem unwilling to do from Jesus and the Apostles that "Evil is impotent and has no power but that which we let it extort from us", and, "I saw that evil was impotent ... and the only weapon of its triumph was the willingness of the good to serve it." (It is this insight that causes Galt to vow to stop the motor of the world by persuading the creators of the world to withhold their sanction, that is, their guilt-driven struggle to make the world a better place through their own efforts.) It needs those who will not "live" at the point of a gun (the promise of financial security and communal approval inside and outside the local church) while their parishioners and those in the largely nominally "Christian" society around them proceed apace to death and judgment.

The church of the Lord Jesus Messiah requires those whose only values worth living and dying for come from the Father whose Son preceded them in death and LIFE. It does not need, and is now dying from, a supposed "altruism" that soothes the spectators at "worship" on Sundays in the name of "seeker sensitivity" or "reaching people" or "helping others" or any one of a dozen other shibboleths designed to mask the search for success and security and temporary relief from pain and inconvenience at the expense of real living. Every Sunday in America (and increasingly around the world) millions sit and stand on cue and wave their hands and move their lips and clap their hands to the beat of culturally conformed and hollowed out "worship" and listen to therapeutic moralism purveyed as the "Gospel" presented in twenty-minute sound bites (or 30-40 minute "performances" repeatedly advocated by one of the most successful of these "communicators") that will not disturb the dead.

Galt, the Christian believer and preacher, might say, cease wrapping the gospel call for repentance in a soft film of a "love" that will not dare to tell the truth for fear of being without a job, no matter that it is defended as actual loving concern for others and their felt needs. In this case the gun being held at the head of preachers and "worship leaders" is a value system based not in the revealed Word and Will of God but a conformity to the expectations of church-goers who pay the bills and give the assurance and approval needed by "leadership" unable to satisfy its own cravings for self-esteem and respectability. Surely you would not do it for the money or the acclaim and approval of peers, or would we? Is there not more than a little of this danger in the attempt to "do church" without discipleship?

166

This pattern is not Life and will not bring it to the dead who sit in pews and chairs and stand and bounce about to the beat of mediocre "rock," while mouthing words no psalmist would think to put on scroll or paper. No life will come to those whose only real reason for attendance is to get the next fix on self-help formulas and personal improvement plans and "principles" for successful living in the family and on the job and in the social climate of the day. There is no life in a "forgiveness" that requires no repentance or change of Lord-ship. That life can only be found in dying the death that He died when He refused to conform to such folkish ways. There is no point in pretending that such a life at the point of a gun is worth living.

Remember that a "church" without discipleship requires the *sanction* (that is, not just complicity reluctantly but participation through love of the thing required) of those who practice and lead in it. Further, it requires their creativity to be channeled into its stream of shallow wanderings through soft meadows of societal conformity to standards of conduct and ways of life that would shame the prophets and apostles that have gone before you, not to mention the man from Nazareth. By all means, its mantra says, do not offend or challenge with the sounds of repentance or the imagery of the Cross, at least not too soon. We must avoid sounding "hateful" lest we be misunderstood. We must maintain the façade of political correctness. We must not thin the crowds by speaking "hard sayings" about munching and crunching flesh and blood (Jn 6:53, 54). We must not confront even the inner circle, willing to go on alone if we must (Jn 6:68-70). That would be egotistical and unloving and hateful and selfish, not to mention impractical and futile and foolish and unsuccessful. Let us instead engage in "feeding the poor," (meeting "felt needs") which Jesus refused to do on demand and found Himself in such conflict that A. T. Robertson headlines that period of His ministry, "The Collapse of the Galilean Campaign" (*Harmony of the Gospels*, John 6). We must ever keep hope that some vestige of the truth will manage to poke a hole in our irrational process and convert the sinner and revive the church without giving "offense" (in the biblical sense) to either. We ignore the unmistakable fact that Jesus was murdered for His words, not his loving deeds (Jn 7:19, 25; 8:37, 40).

This is the altruism that Jesus would not, nor would His converted Apostles, practice to the satisfaction of the crowds or the expectation of religious and governmental authorities. He did not resist, nor did they (after the Resurrection), when he was taken to the tree, but He did not sanction what they did by continuing to live in their world of feigned allegiance to His Father. He told them they were doing only what had been predicted and planned, but He pronounced woe upon them for doing it (Lk 22:22). He loved the cosmos of His Father and gave Himself up for it, but He did not do it willy-nilly for some altruistic entity known as "others." He did it for the Father and those who would be "drawn" to the Father through Him (Jn 3:14, 15; 8:28; 12:32). He enacted a justifying sequence that was the most purposeful and productive act in history, for it actually procured the salvation of souls and preserved their eternal life and initiated the new creation. And all the while He made it plain He would *never* coerce anyone to follow Him. As the personification of Wisdom, He made it unmistakable that those who miss Him sin against themselves, for "all that hate me love death" (Pro. 8:36).

To the modern church we also say, Who is this Jesus Christ you say you serve? Who is this man whom we say went about feeding the poor and healing the sick and somehow got himself crucified? Who is this man whose purpose was to fix everybody's love life and home life, make everyone successful in business and profession, motivate championship performances in athletics, turn people into beauty queens and muscled up hunks, who responds to music suitable for the bluesy angst of the forlorn lover? Who is this "friend" of the disobedient and uncommitted and inactive and unconcerned? Is this the man they crucified between two thieves while his own disciples fled in cowardly fear? Or is it? Who is Jesus Christ? Is He the man who said these words to the crowds with a special eye on his disciples for their future mission (Matthew 10:26-39)?

> 26 "So have no fear of them [those who oppose and persecute], for nothing is covered that will not be revealed, or hidden that will not be known. 27 What I tell you in the dark, say in the light, and what you hear whispered, proclaim on the housetops. 28 And do not fear those who kill the body but cannot kill the soul. Rather fear him who can destroy both soul and body in hell. 29 Are not two sparrows sold for a penny? And not one of them will fall to the ground apart from your Father. 30 But even

the hairs of your head are all numbered. 31 Fear not, therefore; you are of more value than many sparrows. 32 So everyone who acknowledges me before men, I also will acknowledge before my Father who is in heaven, 33 but whoever denies me before men, I also will deny before my Father who is in heaven.

34 "Do not think that I have come to bring peace to the earth. I have not come to bring peace, but a sword. 35 For I have come to set a man against his father, and a daughter against her mother, and a daughter- in- law against her mother- in- law. 36 And a person's enemies will be those of his own household. 37 Whoever loves father or mother more than me is not worthy of me, and whoever loves son or daughter more than me is not worthy of me. 38 And whoever does not take his cross and follow me is not worthy of me. 39 Whoever finds his life will lose it, and whoever loses his life for my sake will find it."

Is He the one who rebuked Simon Peter with these words?

"Get behind me, Satan! You are a hindrance to me. For you are not setting your mind on the things of God, but on the things of man."

24 Then Jesus told his disciples, "If anyone would come after me, let him deny himself and take up his cross and follow me. 25 For whoever would save his life will lose it, but whoever loses his life for my sake will find it. 26 For what will it profit a man if he gains the whole world and forfeits his soul? Or what shall a man give in return for his soul? 27 For the Son of Man is going to come with his angels in the glory of his Father, and then he will repay each person according to what he has done. 28 Truly, I say to you, there are some standing here who will not taste death until they see the Son of Man coming in his kingdom."

If this is the man, Jesus Christ, the American church needs a wake-up call—check your premises!

Epilogue

Reason's last step is the recognition that there are an infinite number of things that stand beyond it. It is merely feeble if it does not go so far as to realize that. –Pascal, *Pensees*

Ayn Rand believed the universe was benevolent because it was rational. She did not allow for the irrational, except as an aberrant quality of the mind of man that was essentially a leftover of some pre-cognitive condition that we might label "stupidity." Because of this "benevolence" she could posit that while one might not actually "know" everything omnisciently, one could be confident in the quest that it would yield to the superior mind at the very least. For those incapable of pressing on to this boundary there was always the sincere desire to know and the willingness to aspire to knowing and achieving creative productivity on the basis of adherence to Aristotelian principle—that is, do not try to live irrationally in a rational universe. Along the way one could admire and be grateful for enjoying the benefits of the lives and minds of those "outliers" (our current term) who are able to benefit all mankind through their superior efforts. To refuse to strive and appreciate is to become a "second-hander," riding the output of the producers without one's own strivings to achieve and create (this term applies also to those who only get their values from others). Those who simply take hand-outs with the help of the collective or from the immediate guilty sanction of the producers are called "moochers" (a generalization with many nuances in the Rand novels), and those who organize coercive efforts to take directly from the producers and give to others and themselves are called "looters." These "second-handers" are the source of evil in the world, and the whole process of constructing an altruistic morality (man must live for others) to justify this transfer of value from the individual to the collective is what's "wrong with the world." The only way out of this labyrinthine "economy" of life (a broader term than mere business) is the willingness of the individual to insist on his or her right to life regardless of the sanction of others. Man/woman must insist on a selfishness that makes one's own rational judgment supreme over the collective. This judgment is, of course, an enlightened one that eschews self-destructive living.

"Benevolence" as a descriptive for a universe that produces as much "stupidity" (evil) as it appears to do seems to be a misnomer, but we will not

170

quibble for the moment. Nevertheless, perhaps the most troubling moment for many, maybe most, critics of Rand's ethical construct is the disaster in the tunnel that takes so many apparently "innocent" people to an early retribution of sorts. This "payback," as we might name it, is severe and unrelenting, and as we have documented in the quotations, is the kind of settling of accounts that disturbs the sensibilities of sophisticates and romanticists and the uncultured alike in all climes and walks of life. Surely this is too much! As the critics have said, "It's hateful!" Rand, however, maintained that she was portraying the reality of the universe we have, not the one we wish it to be. Even the apparently benign lack of decision for or against a monstrous "evil" working itself out in the world has its ultimate, life-or-death, consequences.

Christians who read the story frequently have the same kind of emotions and mixed feelings, and many will conclude that this cannot be a true rendering of the facts in evidence in the world we know. This form of revulsion and incomprehension will be based on the conviction that only someone who espoused atheism and disliked Christianity could posit such outcomes for such benign behavior as those in the train cars exhibited. Yes, real punishment is due those who caused the disaster directly, but those who were simply living out their lives mostly oblivious to the consequences of their presuppositions and mixed decision-making cannot be held accountable--especially in a world where the God of the Bible, Jesus Christ, has revealed the love of God.

It is just at this point where those who call themselves Christian must cease from romantic notions of the nature of God, who reveals Himself in His Son and the written word. The world is in fact benevolent in a biblical way, because the God of the Bible "loves the *cosmos*" (Jn 3:16) in such a way that He "gave His unique and only Son." Those who "believe in Him" receive "life," but those who do not "perish." No alternatives to Jesus for life, period! And the entire Gospel of John is an exposition of what this "believing" business is all about. It is clearly not the mere attendance at church meetings or the praying of a prayer or the signing of a card or talking to a counselor at an 800 number. It is the kind of commitment with which we closed the last chapter. John follows the most famous verse in the Bible we have quoted here with,

18 Whoever believes in him is not condemned, but whoever does not believe is condemned already, because he has not believed in the name of the only Son of God. 19 And this is the judgment: the light has come into the world, and people loved the darkness rather than the light because their works were evil. 20 For everyone who does wicked things hates the light and does not come to the light, lest his works should be exposed. 21 But whoever does what is true comes to the light, so that it may be clearly seen that his works have been carried out in God. (Jn. 3:18-20)

These words express the nature of the benevolence that comes from the love of God. The shorthand proposition here is that everybody on this earth who has not come to Jesus Christ in repentance from sin and faith in His sin-bearing death on a cross is headed into that tunnel of disaster with absolutely no hope of return just as the most evil monsters on earth have gone down it before. There is no remedy. The friendliest, nicest people on earth are headed to the same fate as Hitler and Stalin and Pol Pot and Pontius Pilate and Judas Iscariot, unless and until they make a decisive break with what Paul calls "the law of sin and death" and put their entire confidence and trust for life and death in Jesus Christ to save and preserve them. To know this is to be accountable for it, and the only rational thing to do is seek God through Jesus Christ for salvation from a horrible consequence that comes with inaction. With this principle as a given fact of "life" *and* death in this universe (act quickly or perish) Rand and the Bible and Jesus Christ are in complete agreement.

What Rand would call "stupidity" and "evil" the Bible calls "sin." The Bible says that "sin" precedes "stupidity" and irrationality because it blinds men and women and represents a willful intent to ignore an area of knowledge, God, that is the answer to what is "wrong with the world" and what will make everything "right with the world." Two propositions, both making ultimate claims requiring rational assessment and either-or decisions. Christians need to press the claims of Christ with urgency and sweet reasonableness without being turned off by the stark choices and separations caused by presenting a Gospel that truly saves. The community of those who reject and/or ignore the claims of Christianity about Jesus Christ and His God and Father need to be very clear who and what you are spurning.

CPSIA information can be obtained at www.ICGtesting.com
Printed in the USA
LVOW13s1323090813

347163LV00006B/42/P

9 781480 081741